THE SUNDAY SCHOOL

STEPHEN REXROAT

GOSPEL PUBLISHING HOUSE
SPRINGFIELD, MISSOURI
02-0594

Dedicated to Pat and all my other teachers who have
taught me that people have to know how much you care
before they care how much you know

Library of Congress Catalog Card Number 79-51833
International Standard Book Number 0-88243-594-9
Printed in the United States of America

Foreword

You may find this hard to believe, but when I was a little boy, Christmas was the *second* most exciting day of the year. The really big day on the calendar was always a Sunday—the Sunday on or just after my birthday.

Unless you were lucky enough to grow up in a place like Pratt, Kansas, and to attend a church like the one my father pastored there in the 1940's, you may not understand such logic. But if you ever had the thrill of squeezing seven pennies in your hot little hand, all through a Sunday school opening exercise and class period in anticipation of the birthday offering that was always a part of the closing assembly, you know what I am talking about.

It has been more than 30 years since that special Sunday, but the memory is still strong. It doesn't take much effort on my part to remember the time I squirmed through those last few minutes before the Sunday school secretary made her way down the hall, bell in hand, ringing the classes to a close.

Upstairs, the pianist would take her place at the old upright piano and begin to pound out one of the simple gospel songs which made us know it was time to march into the sanctuary. A visitor might have wondered at our less-than-orderly entrance, but most of us had our own special place to settle into and we did so with remarkable speed. That's because we were

3

anxious for the Sunday school superintendent to get on with the program.

The predictable program usually included a rousing rendition of "I've Got the Sunday School Enthusiasm," complete with actions designed to call attention to the various parts of the body that felt the effects of said enthusiasm. While this was going on, the secretary of our Sunday school would post the numbers for the day on the record board prominently positioned on the front wall of the sanctuary.

Starting with the offering, she would move on to post the attendance of the same Sunday of the year just past. Finally, she posted the all-important attendance for the day. All eyes followed the posting of the report even as our ears were being bombarded with the announcements and folksy comments from the Sunday school superintendent. It seemed my dad watched the board with unusual interest. When the reports were good, he smiled—but I could catch that troubled look on his face when "the bottom dropped out" and we had a low Sunday. It was easy to see he was taking note of the absentees and making plans to call them the very next day. I guess that's why the average attendance figure got better year after year in that church.

But enough of that. Let's get back to that predictable program I was telling you about. The last thing on the agenda was the best—at least as far as those of us who had birthdays to celebrate were concerned. The superintendent would signal the start of the main event by taking a step back from the pulpit. Then, stooping down to look inside the pulpit, he would smile and slowly produce a little white bank in the form of a church. With a sense of ceremony, he would extend the church bank toward us and ask, "Has anyone here had a birthday this week?"

At that magic moment, those who hadn't had a birthday would rubberneck to see if anyone was moving forward. Those of us who had would let a chord or two of "A Happy Birthday to You" be pounded out by the pianist before making our move toward the superintendent, who waited with birthday bank in hand.

Once there, the superintendent would ask you your name, even if you were the pastor's son. Then you got to drop your pennies in one at a time as he carefully counted, and that made it official. The ceremony was sealed by the presentation of a pencil with "Happy Birthday" written on it.

Even the adults would get in on the excitement of that special feature of the Sunday school. The older ones wouldn't give their age away by counting pennies into the bank. They would show off by stuffing a dollar in the bank and then resist the polite pressure of the superintendent to "tell the folks how old" they were. Usually they would keep their secret, but there was one little lady who didn't even try. She would give her dollar and then respond to the superintendent's question with a glowing testimony of God's goodness to her that ended with her stating her age and declaring herself to be that many "years young."

I didn't know her all that well, but I liked her then and I love her now. Her enthusiasm for life and the things of God made it seem she had found the fountain of eternal youth. Come to think of it, I guess she really had.

Researching the material for this book, I came across another birth date. Though not all historians agree, most date the Sunday school movement from 1780 and the first efforts of Robert Raikes.

While pondering the arguments and evidence, I began to daydream. In my thoughts, I was a kid again and I was in the closing assembly of a Sunday school session. I imagined the Sunday school spirit had been personified and was visiting our church that day. When the superintendent asked if anyone had a birthday to celebrate, Mr. Sunday School stood and with great dignity made his way to the front. To the question, "Your name, sir?" he replied, "Mr. Sunday School." When the superintendent asked him if he would mind disclosing his age, he smiled and with a twinkle in his eye, he answered with the question, "Would you believe 200 years young?"

When he said that, the congregation gasped in amazement that anyone so old could be so obviously alive and well. At this point in my imagining, I was enjoying my daydream so much I decided to let it roll on and imagined the spirited song of the congregation as we sang just to him, "A happy birthday to you . . . and the best year you ever had."

I am delighted that 1980 offers us an opportunity to celebrate the founding of the modern Sunday school movement. But more than that, I am celebrating the spirit of Christian concern that has moved great men of God, like Robert Raikes, to begin such evangelistic endeavors.

I am, without apology, a Sunday school enthusiast. I guess I've been one for as long as I can remember. It has been such a blessing to me personally, I want everyone else to be blessed by it. That's why I have written this book. As a result of reading it, I pray you will sense the Sunday school spirit. It may be a page from our past, but it isn't passe. It is a dynamic design for discipling and a strategy of the Spirit for this day and time.

Contents

1
200 or 2,000 Years Young?

Some of the clergy, in different parts of this country, bent upon attempting a reform among the children of the lower class, are establishing Sunday schools, for rendering the Lord's Day subservient to the ends of instruction, which has hitherto been prostituted to bad purposes.

Robert Raikes
Gloucester Journal
November 3, 1783

And he goeth up into a mountain, and calleth unto him whom he would: and they came unto him. And he ordained twelve, that they should be with him, and that he might send them forth to preach, and to have power to heal sicknesses, and to cast out devils.

Mark 3:13-15

How old is the Sunday school movement? Your answer to that question depends on when you start counting. And the point at which you start counting depends on your definition. Historians have haggled over its age for years because they haven't been able to agree on a common list of qualifying factors that earn an attempt at moral education the right to be called a "Sunday school."

Most historians of the Sunday school movement have made the first effort of Robert Raikes in 1780 the bench mark from which they measure. But the claims for earlier persons and places are numerous and so have been the disputes regarding dates and other details.

A strong argument can be made that the basic characteristics of the Sunday school existed before the days of Abraham. Archaeological discoveries have proved that schools existed in Chaldea and Babylonia and tablets revealing information about the religious education methods used in those schools have been found.

According to the Old Testament, Abraham taught those he was responsible for. The Mosaic law required religious education and the prophets were promoters of moral instruction. Reformers like Jehoshaphat recognized the vital role of the religious educator and Nehemiah's record of rebuilding gives a lot of print to Ezra's reading of the Law in the hearing of the people.

Jesus, who as a child was a participant in the Jewish educational system, grew up to become an effective teacher of truth. Even those who deny His claim to deity are more than willing to grant Him the title "Teacher." Thomas Wright paid Him this tribute: "The Sermon on the Mount is Christ's biography. Every syllable He had already written down in deeds. The sermon merely translated His life into language."

Christ's closing command to His students was to go and teach others just as He had taught them and He promised to be with them always in their efforts to evangelize through education.

In the fourth century, Gregory the Illuminator started schools of the Bible for children in Armenia and it is thought that this, more than any other strategy, explains the strength of the Christian church in that place and time. In 680, the Sixth Council of Constantinople called for the establishing of schools in churches with the Bible as the textbook. The importance of the church school was recognized by leaders of the Reformation like Luther, Zwingli, Knox, and Calvin.

Carlo Borromeo, Roman Catholic Archbishop of Milan, gave himself to the teaching of children in an attempt to slow the alarming spread of the reform movement. There followed multiplied efforts to save the children for the Roman Catholic Church through church school instruction.

In America, the Puritans met on Saturday afternoons for religious instruction and there are ample records of "Sunday schools" in many places in America prior to 1780. A casual reading of religious history requires one to face the fact that the Sunday school idea was no instant inspiration.

Throughout the history of the Christian church, attempts to establish such an agency for Biblical instruction are recorded. But these efforts were isolated and the momentum was never maintained sufficiently to produce a mass movement until Robert Raikes popularized the idea through his efforts as a philanthropist and publisher. He certainly deserves the honor we give him as the founder of the modern Sunday school movement.

Before saying more about the history of the movement, I will pause here to make a self-revealing statement regarding the Sunday school. I think it only fair to let you know my personal prejudice in this matter and so I offer my own working definition of a "Sunday school" and then the date I believe it all began.

First, the definition. *A Sunday school is an evangelism-through-education effort.* I'll have a lot more to say on this point in chapters 2 through 5, but for now suffice it to say, the purpose of the Sunday school is evangelism. The salvation of souls and the resulting life change is far more important than the day of the week, methods of the teacher, or organization of the class when it comes to defining Sunday school.

This definition rules out religious education that is not Christian and disqualifies church schools that teach things other than the gospel which the apostle Paul declared to be "the power of God unto salvation" (Romans 1:16). But it does qualify all efforts to obey the Great Commission recorded in Matthew 28:18-20. It really doesn't matter to me the day of the week or the style of the effort as long as it seeks to evangelize through education as Jesus did when He began *discipling* the Twelve.

Now let's set a date for the start of the Sunday school strategy. Actually, I'm not sure of the day, month, or year but I know the moment. It was the moment described in Mark 3:13, 14 when Jesus went "up into a mountain, and calleth unto him whom he would. . . . And he ordained twelve, that they should be with him, and that he might send them forth to preach."

In other words, I believe Jesus to be the founder of the Sunday school movement—a movement that began with His heartbeat of concern for sinners and has continued to be expressed by those who have received Him as Saviour and Lord. I think men like Robert Raikes, William Fox, John Wesley, Count Zinzendorf, and Martin Luther were simply giving expression to the Sunday school spirit. And the Sunday school spirit is a manifestation of the Spirit of God reaching out to reveal himself to man through the Word that became flesh—the Lord Jesus Christ.

Their efforts reveal their personal style and gifts and reflect the times in which they ministered, but there is a marked similarity to be seen in the heroes of the Sunday school hall of fame. Each was aware of God's love and cared about the unloved around him. And each one dared to do what he could to communicate the love of God to all who would hear and heed the gospel.

My definition of a Sunday school and my strong belief that the movement began with the Beginner of all things, Jesus Christ, makes me far more comfortable with a Sunday school starting date that goes back about 2,000 years than the popular bicentennial we will celebrate in 1980. But that doesn't mean I won't join in the celebration of the 200th anniversary of Robert Raikes' first class in "sooty alley." In fact, I think every effort to evangelize through education should be celebrated. If the angels rejoice, why shouldn't we?

From 1780 to 1980

Gloucester, England, during the days of Robert Raikes was anything but a model city. *Deplorable* is a common word used by historians to describe the physical and moral conditions in the city. Housing was crude and offered little comfort. Educational opportunities for the common folk were almost nonexistent and the spiritual climate was pathetic. Vice was a way of life with most of the common class, while the ruling class tried to control the criminals with harsh laws and extreme penalties. Prisons were crammed with a mix of confirmed criminals and those whose only sin against society was their poverty.

Robert Raikes was moved by the misery. He had inherited a tender heart from his publisher father who had tried to help the poor whenever and however he could. He died when Robert was 21 and left him an unfinished task and the ownership of the *Gloucester Journal*.

God's hand on Robert Raikes can be seen in his strategic placement as a publisher. Besides being a philanthropist, he was privileged to have a platform from which to promote his projects. He did not hesitate to call the attention of his readers to the raw side of society and propose plans to deal with the problems he pointed to. His point of view wasn't always popular.

His detractors nicknamed him "Bobby Wild Goose" because they thought some of his suggestions sounded silly.

But Raikes was a patient and persistent man. He worked for almost a quarter of a century with adult criminals before finally facing the fact that he had more often failed than succeeded. At the age of 45, he decided if he was to change society, he would have to start with the children.

His "new experiment" began in Mrs. Meredith's kitchen in a place called Sooty Alley. It was so named because of the chimney sweeps who lived in that area. His first students were from the lowest class of society and were infamous for their cursing and rowdy behavior. During the week, the children were kept hard at work in factories, but on Sundays they spent their time playing, quarreling, and making mischief.

Some of his first students weren't anxious to participate in his great experiment and it is said he had to march a few to class with a wooden log tied to their feet so they couldn't run away. He paid Mrs. Meredith to instruct the children, but they behaved so badly that the first effort had to be ended. He said he found the boys to be "bad and the girls worse" and Mrs. Meredith just couldn't cope. So the class was moved to the kitchen of a Mrs. King and Mrs. Mary Critchley was hired as their new teacher.

The undisciplined children who came to the school ranged from 6 to 14 years of age and the first lesson they all learned well was that Robert Raikes believed in discipline and demanded his rules be obeyed. They had to come to class with clean hands and faces. Their hair had to be combed and they were to wear the best they had. If it wasn't good enough, Robert Raikes bought them better shoes and clothing.

He rewarded well-behaved pupils with Bibles, books, games, and combs, but those who misbehaved were punished. Many were fortunate or unfortunate enough to receive his wrath when they caused trouble. J. Henry Harris, the author of *Robert Raikes—The Man and His Work,* quoted William Brick, a student who reminisced following the funeral of the famous founder:

> I can remember Mr. Raikes well enough. I remember his caning me. I don't suppose I minded it much. He used to cane boys on the back of a chair. Some turrible (sic) bad chaps went to school when I first went. There were always bad 'uns coming in. I know the parents of one or two of them used to walk them to school with fourteen pound weights tied to their legs. . . . Sometimes boys would be sent to school with logs of wood tied to their ankles, just as if they were wild jackasses, which I suppose they were, only worse. When a boy was very bad, he would take him out of the school, and march him home and get his parents to wallop him. He'd stop and see it done, and then bring the urchin back, rubbing his eyes and other places. Mr. Raikes was a terror to all evildoers and a praise to them that did well. Everyone in the city loved and feared him.

After starting several schools in different Gloucester slums and observing that the experiments had been reasonably successful, Robert Raikes decided to take the wraps off his pet project. He was encouraged in this decision by men who shared his burden and vision, like John and Charles Wesley, George Whitefield, William Fox, and William Wilberforce.

The fact he was the publisher of the *Gloucester Journal* made it easy for him to release the news once he decided to do so. November 3, 1783, the paper carried this report:

> Some of the clergy, in different parts of this country, bent upon attempting a reform among the children of

the lower class, are establishing Sunday schools for rendering the Lord's Day subservient to the ends of instruction, which has hitherto been prostituted to bad purposes. Farmers, and other inhabitants of the towns and villages complain that they receive more injury in their property on the Sabbath than all the week besides. This, in a great measure, proceeds from the lawless state of the younger class, who are allowed to run wild on that day, from every restraint.

To remedy this evil, persons duly qualified are employed to instruct those that cannot read; and those that may have learnt to read, are taught the Catechism and conducted to church. By thus keeping their minds engaged, the day passes profitably, and not disagreeably. In those parishes where the plan has been adopted, we are assured that the behavior of the children is greatly civilized.

The barbarous ignorance in which they had before lived, being in some degree dispelled, they begin to give proofs that those persons are mistaken who consider the lower orders of mankind incapable of improvement and therefore think an attempt to reclaim them impractical or, at least, not worth the trouble.

The account was picked up by the London papers and a letter by Raikes was published in *The Gentleman's Magazine* further explaining the project. John Wesley also called attention to the schools through a magazine he edited. This publicity brought a number of inquiries to Robert Raikes and further information was published. His project was praised in many pulpits and the first sign of a mass movement began to appear.

However, not everyone approved. Even some clergymen misunderstood what was happening and to the embarrassment of the church of Christ, whose Spirit was motivating the movement, they spoke out against the idea. A later issue of *The Gentleman's Magazine* carried a slashing attack against the Sunday schools and their founders. A clergyman who used the pen name "Eusebius" expressed his fear that the schools would make the poor unfit for menial service and result in rebellion. His lengthy article concluded:

> We may, therefore, conclude that the Sunday school is so far from being the wise, useful or prudential institution it is said to be, that it is in reality productive of no valuable advantage, but on the contrary, is subversive of that order, that industry, that peace and tranquility which constituted the happiness of society; and that, so far from deserving encouragement and applause, it merits our contempt, and ought to be exploded as the vain commercial institution of a visionary projector.

But Victor Hugo was right when he said there is "nothing in this world more powerful than an idea whose time has come." And the Sunday school idea not only survived the attacks and opposition, it also fed on them and grew great. The uncomplimentary comments only served to call greater attention to the idea, and the enemies of the Sunday school served to call many new friends to the side of Robert Raikes.

The ultimate earthly tribute was paid by the Queen of England when she sent for Robert Raikes; asking to hear from his own lips the story of his schools and the progress to that point. When he died in 1811, Sunday schools in England were well established. Attendance was estimated at 400,000 and he had lived long enough to see his "ragged schools" receive the respect due them. In accordance with his last will and testament, each child present for his funeral received a schilling and a plum cake. Even in death, he expressed the Sunday school spirit of concern for children.

An Idea That Became an Institution

The year 1736 witnessed not only the birth of Robert Raikes, but also the appearance of William Fox on the stage of human history. Although they were not acquainted during their early years, their two great efforts for the glory of God and good of mankind eventually brought them together. Even with his paper as a platform and his passion for evangelism through education, it is doubtful Robert Raikes could have launched the modern Sunday school movement without the cooperation of William Fox and the influential Sunday School Society he founded.

William Fox was a rich merchant in London who believed society could only be bettered through a national Bible-reading effort. As he traveled from village to village, he was appalled at the absence of Bibles and greatly disturbed to discover that even when Bibles were given, only 1 in 20 was able to read them. His great desire was expressed in the statement of purpose, ". . . that every poor person in the kingdom might be able to read the Bible."

In 1785, he founded an organization that was at first called "The Society for the Support and Encouragement of Sunday School in the Different Counties of England." When the effort was expanded to include Wales, Ireland, and the British Colonies, the name of the organization was changed to "The Society for the Support and Encouragement of Sunday Schools throughout the British Dominions." Mercifully, the title was reduced through common usage to simply "The Sunday School Society."

Other Sunday school societies followed and the idea grew beyond local limits. Even the churches began to show interest in the endeavor and on July 13, 1803, William Brodie Gurney and a few friends founded the London Sunday School Union. The founding meeting was held in Surrey Chapel where Rowland Hill was the pastor. The goals of the founders were to stimulate and encourage the religious education of the young, improve methods of instruction, promote the opening of new schools, and furnish inexpensive literature to Sunday schools. The organization experienced a slow but sure growth; producing publications, forming auxiliaries, developing plans for better Sunday school buildings, and promoting teacher training through classes, publications, and a teacher-training college.

Meanwhile, in the United States, conditions were much like those in England. In spite of the revivals of colonial times, atheism and wickedness thrived. The emphasis on education had declined and the French influence was against Christianity. The catechism was about all there was to offer the children and preachers knew only one educational strategy—the sermon. So the children's Christian education suffered from neglect.

From 1785 until the early 1800's a few Sunday schools based on the British model were begun. In 1790, a transdenominational group in Philadelphia formed the "First Day or Sabbath School Society" for the purpose of instructing children by teaching from the "Bible and from such other moral and religious books as the society might, from time to time direct."

The Sunday school endeavors existed outside the organized church for several years, but after 1810 a few congregations began to offer the use of church facilities as free meeting places. After the War of 1812, the Sunday school idea spread rapidly in cities, towns, and villages. Support organizations began to be formed but the schools, for the most part, were still forced to operate independent of organized churches because no denomination really got behind the endeavor.

Eventually, denominational efforts did develop. In

1827, the Methodists formed the General Sunday School Society. In 1830, the Lutherans, and in 1832, the Congregationalists made similar moves. It was in 1832 that the first national Sunday school convention was held in Philadelphia. A great part of the growth of the Sunday school movement can be traced to this technique for informing and inspiring the Christian community regarding the Sunday school.

After 7 years of foundational work, on May 25, 1824, the American Sunday School Union was formed. The founding of the union was an important event in the history of the United States as well as the Sunday school movement. The American Sunday School Union made a tremendous contribution to the development of the moral value system of the young and westward-growing nation.

In 1830, the American Sunday School Union accepted the challenge of "within two years, and in reliance upon divine aid to establish a Sunday school in every destitute place where it is practical, throughout the Valley of the Mississippi." The records of the union regarding the "valley campaign" are delightful to read and one is most impressed by the great faith and confidence of those who accepted the call to a parish that extended from Harrisburg, Pennsylvania, to the Rocky Mountains and from Canada to the Gulf of Mexico.

A young fur trader wrote to his mother in Connecticut from St. Louis shortly after the 1830 "valley campaign" was started. The letter, now a part of the St. Louis History Collection of the Missouri State Historical Society, gives us a glimpse of one man's excitement during those days. Listen to his unedited enthusiasm.

We are fast growing to a giant's stature. The days of our childhood will soon be past. If nothing but the love of country actuate us something must be done to dispel

ignorance and drive away vice. So thought the members
of the General Assembly when they lately met in Philadelphia. They were, however, inspired by higher mo-
tives. The glory of God and the love of souls influenced
them. Later, they passed a resolution to establish Sunday schools in every settlement in this valley, within the
short space of two years; a resolution fraught with greater
consequences to the Nation than any ever before adopted.

But why am I speaking of these things? An excitement
has gone forth. An excitement that the power of man can
neither gainsay or put down. It exists not in the East alone.
It has passed the boundary which separates the East
from the Western States. It has reached this place.

Can teachers but be found to take charge of these
schools as they are formed, we may soon hope a different state of things. Sabbath Schools are the only means
which the great majority of the people of this State have
for the education of their children, and unless these
schools are established, books given them, and adequate
teachers found to take charge of them, we cannot expect
the children will be any better than their Fathers were.
Think it then, My dear Mother, no hardship that you are
separated thus far from one of your children but rather
rejoice that he is permitted to come and be in some hum-
ble part in this great work.

One of the many Sunday school missionaries sent
out by the Sunday School Union was a man named
Stephen Paxson. His parish was the frontier between
the Allegheny and Rocky Mountains, and he covered
his territory on the back of a trusty horse he called
Robert Raikes. His record still stands as an inspiration
to those who labor for the Lord. During his ministry,
he organized 1,314 Sunday schools with a total enrollment of 83,405 students. All of this was the result of
one man's obedience to the Great Commission and an
expression of the Sunday school spirit.

Entering the 1900's the story of the Sunday school
is one of "good news" and "bad news." The good news

is the new century began with the Sunday school movement in what one historian called its "golden age." Enrollment figures showed that in North America alone nearly 20 million students were enrolled. But the bad news was to follow when, in 1916, the movement began to decline in attendance. Government figures showed that between 1926 and 1936 there was a 12.6-percent decline in enrollment. Interestingly, during the days of the "great decline" the Assemblies of God Sunday schools showed a 300-percent increase.

D. V. Hurst, a contributor to a 1957 Assemblies of God text titled *Operation Sunday School*, said:

> From its early foundation, the Assemblies of God has stressed the Sunday school idea. As early as 1914, Mrs. J. R. Flower prepared lesson comments on the International Sunday school lessons for publication in the *Evangel*.

In 1934, the denomination printed a study manual by Ralph M. Riggs, titled *A Successful Sunday School*. District directors and traveling representatives played a key role in exciting the churches of the movement concerning the Sunday school. A most significant and successful strategy was the Sunday school convention. The number of delegates grew until in the 10th convention, 9,218 delegates registered; breaking all known attendance records for Sunday school conventions.

The recent history of the Sunday school movement is recorded in the periodicals and publications of hundreds of denominations and many major publishing houses. Much of it is too recent to risk rushing to conclusions about. But I think it is safe to say that wherever you find people who take seriously the Great Commission, there you find the Sunday school alive and well. The style may be changing, but the strategy is still evangelism through education.

My review of the history of the happening we call the Sunday school movement causes me to concur with the young fur trader and Sunday school enthusiast whose letter I quoted earlier. He said it all when he reported: "An excitement has gone forth" and that excitement "has reached this place."

It is an excitement that has been going forth for a long time now and I'm convinced it will continue until the second coming of Jesus Christ rings the "school's out" bell.

I began this chapter with the question, "How old is the Sunday school?" I suppose you will have to decide for yourself which date—if there is a set date—you are most comfortable with. So what do you say? Is it 200 years old, having begun in 1780 with Robert Raikes' first ragged school? Or did Jesus start it all when He called His first class of 12 to order about 2,000 years ago? Or, could it be neither answer is really right and the Sunday school spirit is as eternal as the Spirit of the eternal God? After all, it was His love for us that caused Christ to come as the Word that became flesh and dwelt among us. John 3:16 explains it this way: "For God so loved the world, that he gave his only begotten Son, that whosoever believeth in him should not perish, but have everlasting life."

So try to date the beginning of God's love for man and maybe you will be able to answer the question I asked. But if you can't, don't let it bother you. Just rejoice that you know God's love is "now" and the excitement that has gone forth "has reached this place" and time.

2
The Master's Plan

This is at once the glory and the power of Christianity.
Christ changes ordinary men into supernatural men.
                                                A. P. Gouthey

And Jesus, walking by the Sea of Galilee, saw two
brethren, Simon called Peter, and Andrew his brother,
casting a net into the sea: for they were fishers. And he
saith unto them, Follow me, and I will make you fishers
of men. And they straightway left their nets, and followed him.

                                         Matthew 4:18-20

Luke, the author, began his second book with a ref-
erence to his masterpiece and the Master's plan it revealed: "The former treatise have I made,
O Theophilus, of all that Jesus began both to do and
teach."

The second book became necessary because in the
first one the story had just been started. The Book of
Acts was not a sequel for the sake of cashing in on
the success of an earlier effort. Luke had to pick up
his pen again because the story of Jesus was a story
that just kept growing and demanded more space. So
he wrote the story of God's "possibility" people and
gave us a glimpse of the glory revealed through common folk who were changed by the teaching of Jesus,
the Master Teacher.

Even the Book of Acts wasn't big enough to tell the

whole story. That may explain why Luke left it open-ended and did not put an "amen" at the end like he did when he finished his first book. Perhaps he realized Jesus is truly the Great Beginner and once He starts something it cannot be stopped. There are only 28 chapters in Acts, but the story is still being written. Each generation of believers has added its own testimony to the faithfulness and power of God. As long as He leaves us here, we must assume He still has something to "do" and "teach" through us.

Transformation Through Teaching

Jesus' strategy was to transform through teaching. Rejecting political power and military force, He chose to change things by changing people and He knew the only way to do that was to start with the heart.

Nicodemus recognized Jesus as a teacher of extraordinary ability, so he said, "Thou art a teacher come from God" (John 3:2). Any student of the Bible will understand how and why Nicodemus came to that conclusion. The profound truths taught by this Carpenter from Nazareth were powerful enough to make His listeners sit up and take notice. And what He did to those who followed Him proved positively that He was linked with the living God. He took a bunch of losers and turned them into winners. Men who had been just fishermen became fishers for men and won a following that was phenomenal.

The amazing thing is He did such a great thing in such a quiet way. A few friends became disciples and then those disciples became apostles who represented a heavenly Kingdom and did the sort of things Jesus had done as a demonstration of His deity. Those miracles, performed through the lives of ordinary men made extraordinary by the power of God resident in them, proved a point. God had chosen to share himself with mere men. Those who accepted the teaching of this truth were privileged to become the sons of God.

Recognizing that those who would respond in faith would be a mighty minority, John in the first chapter of his Gospel observed: "He came unto his own, and his own received him not. But as many as received him, to them gave he power to become the sons of God, even to them that believe on His name" (John 1:11, 12).

Galileo is reported to have said: "You cannot teach a man anything; you can only help him find it for himself." Dr. Henrietta Mears' famous maxim, "A teacher has not taught until the learner has learned," says much the same thing. Jesus certainly understood the principle proposed by these famous teachers. He was a most effective learning leader and the success He enjoyed with His disciples makes it plain He understood truth and how to bring men to an understanding of it.

He led His men to a confrontation with the failure of their own efforts and then faced them with the fact that God had reached out to them through Him. Those who discovered that reality became disciples, and those who became disciples were changed for time and eternity. As Gouthey said: "This is at once the power and glory of Christianity. Christ changes ordinary men into supernatural men."

Luke, in the opening lines of Acts, points out a two-part plan for moving men from the natural realm to the supernatural reality. The first part is described by the little word *do* and the second is detailed by the word *teach*. The first section of the statement relates to who Jesus was and what He did, while the second part shows how He enabled others to do the same things.

The gospel begins with the reality that Jesus is the

Christ, the Son of God. This fact He demonstrated by what He did. His manners, message, and miracles were evidences of His claim to be more than a man. Napoleon Bonaparte considered the evidence and then concluded:

> I know men and I tell you that Jesus Christ is no mere man. Between Him and every other person in the world there is no possible term of comparison. Alexander, Caesar, Charlemagne, and I have founded empires. But on what did we rest the creations of our genius? Upon force. Jesus Christ founded His empire upon love; and at this hour millions of men would die for Him.

By what He did, Jesus proved who He was. So Luke remarked about the remarkable things He began to "do." Then, on what was probably the same line, he wrote "and teach." I am glad he said that because it reveals that Jesus came to do something more than demonstrate divine power. He came to reproduce that power in and through those who would trust Him as Saviour and Lord.

Acts 1:8 records His promise: "But ye shall receive power, after that the Holy Ghost is come upon you." This verse goes on to promise they would use their newfound power to witness worldwide. What is suggested is they would do for others what He had done for them. Matthew 28:19 is explicit on this point. It tells us Jesus commanded His disciples: "Go ye therefore, and teach all nations." *The Living Bible* says it this way: "Go and make disciples in all the nations."

Now the Master's plan becomes clear. Do you see it? He came to change men who would, in turn, change other men. The Word of God became flesh that men of flesh might receive the Word of God. Through a process called discipling, He invaded their beings and they began to behave in a different way. So I say it again: His strategy was to transform through teaching.

"A teacher," said Henry Adams, "affects eternity; he can never tell where his influence stops." Of course, he was speaking of mere mortals when he said that. Jesus knew the end from the beginning and His efforts were based on more than hope. He knew the end He desired would be realized as the result of His teaching. Even when He started, He had confidence in His strategy. He knew His game plan would win. Evidence of this is found in His promise to His disciples that they would do even greater things than He had done.

But Mr. Adams' point concerning the far-reaching influence of a teacher is well taken. Jesus surely started something that hasn't stopped.

Following the release of *Roots*, Alex Haley's bestseller about his heritage, many Americans began to research their own personal history. I didn't bother with my family tree but I did wonder a bit about my spiritual family line. I am really intrigued by the question: "Which disciple was it whose ministry of discipling linked me directly with the Lord Jesus Christ?" I confess I don't have the slightest idea which one of the 11 faithful disciples was directly responsible for linking me with my Lord, but this much I know: One of them was obedient to the divine directive and discipled someone, who discipled someone, who discipled someone, until finally someone discipled me.

That was the Master's plan from the beginning and I'm sure glad He started something that brought me to a saving knowledge of himself. By the "doing" and "teaching" Luke referred to, Jesus discipled the Twelve and, through them, all those who follow in their footsteps. Discipling was the Master's plan and still is the salvation strategy of the Church He founded. Matthew 28:18-20 makes us know His will for our work. It's the mandate under which we minister, and just in case you haven't read it recently, here it is again:

> Go ye therefore, and teach all nations, baptizing them in the name of the father, and of the Son, and of the Holy Ghost: teaching them to observe all things whatsoever I have commanded you: and, lo, I am with you alway, even unto the end of the world. Amen (Matthew 28:19, 20).

That popular word, *discipling,* has come to common usage only recently. I can't recall hearing it used to describe the process of evangelism through education during my days as a ministerial student. Even though the college I attended was founded for the purpose of "training ministers, missionaries, and Christian workers," the term *discipling* wasn't used by those who were discipling me—at least as far as I can recall. In those days, we stayed with the standard King James term *teach,* and one of my classes was called Principles of Teaching. It might just as well have been called Details of Discipling but, like I said, in those days we didn't use that term.

Recently we have been hearing more and more about the discipling aspects of preaching and teaching. The church-growth movement has stressed that there is more to preaching than a platform, pulpit, and preacher and true teaching is tested by the life change it effects in the learner.

I recently listened uncomfortably to charges made by a minister against a media ministry. He charged "fraud" because some of the converts the ministry claimed had not demonstrated significant life change and the media effort seemed to him more intent on keeping count than conserving the convert and developing disciples. His "fraud" charge was based on the fact the program was using the number of phone calls to conclude its ministry was supereffective and should therefore receive the support of the audience. What made me uncomfortable was the charge and the knowledge that we have too often been pushed by the cult of success to count converts at the point of "I see that hand" decisions rather than when they accept the disciplines of discipleship and make a commitment to a community of believers called a church.

Evangelism that does not produce disciples is at best an incomplete effort and at worst a fraud of the most awful sort. Decisions begin the discipling process, but that is only a start. That is when the effort must really begin. In his book *Your Church Can Grow* (Glendale, CA: G/L Regal Publications, 1976), Peter Wagner lists seven signs of a vital church. The sixth sign, according to Wagner, is an evangelistic method that works. His definition of a method that works is one that results in disciples, not just decisions.

Discipling Discovered

The first time I remember hearing the word was in 1967 while pastoring in Newcastle, Wyoming. Dr. and Mrs. Melvin Hodges, noted Assemblies of God missionaries and former pastors of the church, had returned to minister to the congregation. They observed a ministry we had started to the church youth that involved weekly fellowship and training sessions and culminated in a work-and-witness field trip. Mrs. Hodges seemed excited by what she saw and said something to her husband about our "discipling" the youth of the church. I had a general idea what she meant, and it was obvious to me by the way she said it the word was a positive and powerful one.

A short time later, Eva Davison, a delightful and gifted missionary, was a guest speaker in the church and we were in the final stages of preparation for our summer field trip with the youth. She too seemed most interested in what was happening and like the lady before her, she used that word—*discipling*. This time I asked for a definition and she started my study of a concept that has changed my mind and ministry.

She explained that "discipling" was simply the process Jesus used in the development of disciples. Sharing her insights into the transformation of the Twelve through the teaching/discipling of Jesus, she showed me how He had trained a team for the task of world evangelism. When our conversation ended, I was convinced discipling was much more than one of the things the church should be doing—it was the total task of the church of Jesus Christ in the world today.

After she left our little town, she was scheduled to preach in Cheyenne. Since it was on the road to our mission project, we decided to stop and hear her again. Perhaps she sensed my hunger to know more about discipling or maybe God told her to tell me the things she shared in her sermon—I really don't know. But I do know what I heard her say that night has had more influence on my philosophy and style of ministry than any other single experience I have had. There were no spiritual fireworks that night, no mystical experience I was aware of; just three words that outlined the discipling process—*inspiration, instruction,* and *involvement.*

The Tri-I Concept

It has been several years since my encounter with that dynamic lady and the word she explained to me is still being studied. The more light that shines on it, the more it sparkles, and the more I realize its value. Somewhere between then and now, I began to explain my philosophy of the ministry and discipling as the Tri-I Concept.

This basic belief was founded on the first fact of the lordship of Christ. Then came the truth that the only normative response to the lordship of Christ is the discipleship of believers. Finally, I told those who would listen that according to Matthew 28:18-20, the mission of the church is the making of disciples and this is accomplished through a ministry that mimicks the methods of Jesus—*inspiration, instruction,* and *involvement.*

Not everyone has seen it my way, but many have shared my excitement and a long list of ministry efforts based on this philosophy have tested the concept and proved it powerful. Where there have been failures, the reason has not been the strategy, but my human efforts in implementing it. And the successes have proved Jesus knew what He was doing when He ordered His church to go and make disciples.

Having tried and tested this concept as a pastor and director of Christian education, I am prepared to argue that every effort we make as Christian communicators must seek to incorporate the Tri-I principles. They are the tripod on which our Sunday school stands and they are also obvious in our worship services and auxiliary efforts. We seek to obey the Great Commission and are guided by the Tri-I Concept because it is the way Jesus worked and in 2,000 years there hasn't been a better idea.

Discipling Defined

When asked to give my working definition of the term *discipling,* I say: "Discipling is the proclamation of the gospel in the dual forms of declaration and discipline; resulting in the establishment and enrichment of a relationship between a believer and the Lord Jesus Christ."

This definition covers more than the post-evangelism part of the process. I argue that discipling begins when a discipler first reaches out to a prospective disciple. I believe Jesus began the discipling of Levi and all the others when He said to them, "Follow Me." To those who think the discipling ministry is undertaken once the evangelist has snared the sinner, I say, "Look again." Discipling is the total process of evangelism and education.

Once the initial relationship has been established between the new believer and his Lord, a continuing effort to strengthen and enrich the relationship must be undertaken. This is accomplished through Christian fellowship, guided Bible study, and prayer. Once the inspiration of the Holy Spirit has brought an awareness of the presence of Christ in the life, faithful instruction must begin to establish the believer in his newfound faith.

A Definition of the Details

Now let's look at those three important words—*inspiration, instruction,* and *involvement*—and attempt to define them.

The word *inspiration* is defined by the physician as "the drawing of air into the lungs" or "inhalation." The preacher usually uses the word to describe a "divine influence directly exerted on the mind or soul of a man." I like to think of it as describing the state of being alive. After all, when we talk about someone expiring, don't we mean he has died? Then doesn't the opposite word, *inspire,* suggest a state of life?

I believe when Jesus Christ is communicated by the Holy Spirit to a human heart, new life begins. Jesus described the work of the Spirit as a wind that moves where it will, and He likened the life change of Christian conversion to being "born again."

The man who heard Him say that was mystified by the statement. And so are most of us when it comes to understanding the wondrous way the Lord lets His life flow into our life. But even if we can't fully understand it, we can know it has happened as His Spirit bears witness with our spirit that we have become the children of God.

To be inspired as a disciple of Jesus Christ is to be inbreathed by His presence and power; to let His life begin to be within you. The hymn writer was obviously inspired when he penned the words, "You ask me how I know He lives; He lives within my heart."

Inspiration is a wonderful thing, but in the disciple's experience it isn't the only thing. Jesus not only moved men by the power of His presence, He also grounded them in the truth He taught. Once a disciple had been inspired to follow Jesus, the instruction began. He lectured, told stories, and used field trips to teach eternal truth.

Jesus *instructed* His disciples about himself and themselves. He helped them understand their relationship with their Father in heaven and the purpose of life on planet earth. He taught them how to minister and dealt with all the details, even down to telling them how to pack for their travels and how to handle rejection by those who refused His truth. Jesus taught His disciples so His disciples might teach others, and even today the process continues.

An exciting discovery is being made by those who watch churches grow. They are seeing that promotion and "hype" seem to be giving way to "worship and the Word of God." In other words, the great churches of today are rediscovering the dynamics of discipling and finding the teaching of God's Word is a powerful part of building a great body of believers.

This brings us to that third word—*involvement*. The result of instruction is involvement. Leadership development results in leadership and it is exciting to see the liberation of the laity in the church world today. This is more than another emphasis or program of the church. This is a part of the Master's plan and there is a lot more to be said about it in chapter 3. But for now, know this: the only adequate response to the massive needs of mankind is the ministry of Jesus Christ, multiplied through those who have been inspired and instructed and will get involved. We must recognize God likes help when helping people and pray like St. Francis of Assisi, "Lord, make me an instrument of your peace."

We may not fully understand why, but it is obvious Christ has chosen to work through human hands. He has no new plan for the 20th century. He still wills to work through those willing to be inspired, instructed, and involved. In 2,000 years there hasn't been a better idea and it is still the Master's plan.

3
Called to Communicate

To get an idea across, wrap it up in a person.
Ralph Bunche

And he said unto them, Go ye into all the world, and preach the gospel to every creature.
Mark 16:15

Make no mistake about it, we are called to communicate. The Great Commission is crystal clear on this point. Although Matthew and Mark used different words, there is no disagreement on the big idea. Jesus commanded His disciples to continue to communicate the good news of God's love.

Matthew used the word *matheteuo*, which the King James Version translates "teach," and "preach" is used to translate Mark's choice, *kerusso*. *The Living Bible* uses the word *disciple* in place of teach, but still the big word behind all these words is *communicate*.

The same idea is evident in the words of promise recorded in Acts 1:8. Remember the passage? Jesus had just promised His disciples power as the result of the coming of the Holy Spirit upon them. Then He matter-of-factly mentions the purpose of that power will be realized as they become "witnesses" in Jerusalem, Judea, Samaria, and around the world. Of course the promise was kept, and on the Day of Pentecost the Church became a witnessing community which continues to this day to minister under this mandate of the Master.

It is commonly called the Great Commission and indeed it is. By commanding His disciples to do what He had done, He made them partners in a project that is greater than our human understanding can grasp. God was declaring His grace and glory to the world through Jesus Christ while He was here in physical form. Now He is making Him known through the Church, which serves as the body of Christ in the world today. The last recorded words of Jesus make it plain the purpose of His new body (the Church) is proclamation. He created and called us to be communicators.

Communicate

The list of words that spin off the word *communicate* is a long one in my thesaurus. And the countless texts on the subject of communication remind us the idea suggested by the word isn't as simple as it sounds at first hearing. When you put a snowflake under a microscope, you see much more than a small white blob of moisture. The closer look reveals a beautiful and complex work of art that shows the creativity of God. The same is true when you place the word *communicate* under the careful scrutiny of the student of communication theory.

We are told the purpose of communication is to transfer a concept from a sender to a receiver. Perfect communication is achieved when meaning matches meaning. But many students of the science argue such a perfect transaction has never taken place. Given the problems involved in sending and receiving the message, it is hard to argue with their conclusion and we are generally content to just get close enough to count.

When verbal communication becomes confusing,

we suggest the communicator "put it in writing," but even the written word can confuse. For example, take the experience of a convention planner. He had contacted a sign painter in preparation for a large convention several years ago. His written order directed that delegate areas be marked by 50 signs that were to be printed with "the 48 states plus Alaska and Hawaii." To his dismay, he got exactly what he asked for—50 neatly printed signs each carrying the message: "The 48 states plus Alaska and Hawaii."

Whether the sign painter produced the placards as a prank to underscore the ambiguous language of the order, or he was just mindlessly following directions, I don't know. I do know that the man who explained his black eye by saying he had misunderstood his wife's order to "shut up" as a command to "stand up" was just joking. But the problems produced by faulty communications aren't to be laughed off.

How often have you heard major marital problems dismissed as simply a "communication breakdown"? Isn't the generation gap more accurately defined as a communication gap? And how much is the cost to industry for the problems produced because employees can't seem to communicate clearly with one another? One wit put the frustrations of confused communicators into this silly sentence: "I know you think you heard what I said, but I'm not sure you understand that what I meant to say was not exactly what you thought you heard."

The science and art of communication is easy to define, but not so easy to do. That is because the definition is simple but it covers a multitude of complexities not at first noticed by the student of communication.

To communicate is, according to *The Random House Dictionary of the English Language:* "To impart knowledge of; make known; give to another; impart; transmit."

My definition is even more simple. I say that to communicate is to "pass it on." By that, I mean you move something from point A to point B. For example, you can communicate this book to someone else by handing or mailing it to him. And what is a communicable disease but a sickness you can share with a friend? You can even pass along an idea by putting it into words and moving it from your mind to the minds of others.

What's more, I believe you and I can communicate the very life of the Lord Jesus Christ. The same Holy Spirit who makes us know His presence within us can and will move Him from our life to other lives as we open up to them. The life of Jesus Christ is contagious and those who have been discipled become disciplers —communicators of the life of the Lord Jesus. They are the "pass it on" people who become the living links through which the living presence of Christ is communicated.

My "pass it on" definition might impress you as too simplistic, but before you reject my thoughts on the subject, let me discuss with you some theories concerning communications. I want to do this for a couple of reasons. First, I want you to know I've done my homework and taken a long look at the available ideas and information in the field of communication studies. Second, I need to lay a foundation for my concluding contention, which is: discipling is the ultimate communication design.

There is far too much material on the subject of communication to allow even an overview of all of it. Things like kinesics, mental telepathy, and cognitive dissonance will have to be ignored if I am to obey the good advice embodied in my wife's favorite formula— K.I.S.S. (Keep It Simple Stephen). So, let's just look at the theories and then I will make my observations and argument.

As I see it, there are two basic theories. The one is called the *transportation* theory and the other is referred to as the *resonance* theory. They are not contradictory but compatible, and they complement each other. The big difference between them is one is sight-oriented while the other takes its language from a "sound" vocabulary.

The *transportation* theory is message-centered and works well when charting the movement of information from sender to receiver. It is concerned with message units and their movement. It is print-oriented and takes a line-upon-line approach to the movement of messages.

On the other hand, the *resonance* theory is sound-based. Its understanding of communication is built on the idea of a broadcast voice that is sent out in a circular pattern. It is a theory that has greater relevance to the communication process in the small group or village atmosphere where people see and speak to one another, than to the scattered society that finds it necessary to send signals to its members through smoke, semaphore, or the printed page.

The theory that works best depends on the situation. If the communicators are separated by distance, then the transportation theory makes sense. But when people are communicating face-to-face, the ideas of the resonance theory are more relevant.

The transportation theory gives us the classic model made up of three parts—sender, channel, and receiver. The movement of the message, at least as far as one message unit is concerned, is an eight-part process that involves:

1. An idea the sender wants to share.

2. The coding of said idea into symbols—usually words.

3. The sending of those symbols.

4. The medium or channel along which the symbols flow (printed page, spoken word, signal flags, etc.).

5. The reception of the symbols by the receiver.

6. The decoding of the symbols by the receiver.

7. The realization and response to the idea received.

8. The evaluation by the sender of the receiver's response to the idea.

The big idea is for the meaning of the sender to match the meaning of the receiver. Usually it takes more than one message unit to bring the sender and receiver even close to a common understanding.

The transportation theory has made a tremendous impact on our thinking about communications. The printed page has been primary in our lives for many years and we have come to greatly respect it. It hasn't been all that long ago that something was made certain if you "read it in the paper." Common sayings also reveal how much the idea at the base of the transportation theory has affected us. For example, we declare something to be as simple as "ABC" and brag that we can read someone "like a book."

The changing of our ideas about communication is reflected in the talk of today. Now it is not uncommon to hear someone say he is getting "good vibes" from someone else. Instead of saying, "I see what you mean," you may now hear some say, "I hear you," in response to a point a speaker has made. Both statements mean, "I understand," but each reflects a subtle difference in our way of talking about communication.

The changes are natural responses to our changing social structure. In the early days there wasn't much study of communication—people just communicated face-to-face. But with the separations caused by a frontier movement, other forms of communication were needed and the moving of messages became a complex challenge. One of the assumptions of the traditional transportation theory is that the movement of a message is made difficult by the resistance it encounters at each stage of its passage in a time and space environment.

Radio, television, and other technical advances have removed some of the problems our forefathers faced, and now we find ourselves moving back toward a face-to-face, village environment. The world is fast becoming a global village and almost constant communication is present in our environment.

This means the resonance theory has something to say to us about total communication. We are like 24-hour-a-day radio stations and our signal never stops beeping forth. This idea is more mysterious than the print-oriented transportation theory, but it is also far more powerful. When you grasp the truth that you are the medium which has become the message, you will really begin to be heard "loud and clear."

The Word Becoming Flesh

"To get an idea across," said Ralph Bunche, "wrap it up in a person."

John lets us know God did just that when "the Word [became] flesh, and dwelt among us, (and we beheld his glory, the glory as of the only begotten of the Father,) full of grace and truth" (John 1:14).

This brings me to my belief that discipling is the ultimate communication design. I believe this because the relationship between the discipler and disciple involves a resonance-type communication on the verbal, visual, and vital levels. Look at Jesus with the Twelve. He changed them by what He said to them, what He showed to them, and what He shared with them of His own life and Spirit.

Jesus, who was the Word become flesh, one day told His disciples He would be *in* them just as He was then with them. This reality was realized on the Day of Pentecost when the presence and power of God filled their lives to overflowing. When that happened, they became more than messengers. They became the message that moved men. Eternal truth was not only on their lips, it was also in their lives and they communicated on the verbal, visual, and vital levels.

The same sort of communication must take place in our churches and Sunday schools if lives are to be changed by the power of God. We must speak with our lives as well as our lips if we are to clearly communicate Christ.

Christian communication is the proclamation of the living Word (Jesus) through the written Word (Bible) by the spoken word (human utterance).

I believe people don't change until they receive the living Word. For this to happen, Christian communicators like you and me must pass Him on to them. In other words, we who know Him must make Him known through our lives. We do this through verbal, visual, and vital communications. It is not so much a matter of preaching rules and regulations, but of establishing a relationship that communicates on all three levels—verbal, visual, and vital. That's why I say preaching at its best, teaching at its best, and communication at the ultimate level is better called discipling.

Three Levels of Communication

Verbal Communication

Speech is a grand gift from God and we appreciate the ability it gives us to express ourselves. The tongue of man is recognized as a tremendous tool that must be used for good and the glory of God. One way to do that is to witness by what we say to the goodness and grace of God in our own life and call others to consider what He has to offer them.

Granted, what we say is the lowest rung on the ladder in our climb to communicate, but without it the process would not get off the ground. Our faith must not only be demonstrated, it must also be explained. We must be prepared to obey the scriptural command concerning the giving of a "reason of the hope that is in [us]" (1 Peter 3:15).

Because we are called to be communicators and because speech is so important to our communicating, I urge you to make an all-out effort toward excellence in this area. Study, practice, and work with this gift God has given you. You may never be the best, but you can always become better.

Those who hear you have the right to expect you to do your best verbally. This means you must work at the preparation of the truth you will present and practice, practice, practice the presentation before you make it. There is no excuse for faulty preparation and it will be evident if there has not been proper planning. Either you will sweat in getting your presentation ready or your hearers will sweat when you make it.

My folks used to tell me, "Anything worth doing is worth doing well." I've found myself saying that to my own son a lot lately. And now I'm repeating it to you. Don't you think the declaration of the good news about Jesus Christ deserves our very best effort?

Visual Communication

I remember a Sunday school song from my childhood that warned, "What you do speaks so loud, that the world can't hear what you say." There is a lot of truth in that line and every Christian communicator needs to be reminded now and then that what we do is more powerful than what we say.

Acts begins with Luke's statement concerning what Jesus came to "do" and "teach." The order is significant. Before Jesus explained the divine life, He demonstrated it. He was a walking sermon as well as a teller of truth.

The Sunday school teacher who verbally urges his students to be faithful to the church on Sunday morning, but doesn't show up for the evening meeting is like a teacher who writes with chalk in one hand and an eraser in the other, taking off the board what he just put on.

Jesus inspired people by what He said and He instructed them by the life He lived. To the disciples, His invitation was not, "Listen to me"; it was, "Follow me." This "do as I do" approach produced disciples whose impact is still being felt today.

Vital Communication

Finally, the Christian communicator must recognize the power of nonverbal, nonvisual communication. We communicate by what we say (verbal level) and what we do (visual level), but most of all we communicate by what we are. This vital level of communication is one best understood by those of us who accept and appreciate the power of the Holy Spirit at work in and through us.

This is a level of communication that is just now beginning to enjoy respectability in the field of communication studies. Classes on the power of love to communicate and a growing awareness of the spiritual nature of man are producing some exciting breakthroughs. But it is really nothing new. People who have accepted what God has said about man have known this all along.

I certainly don't understand all I know about how the living Jesus moves through me into others, but I do know I communicate Him by what I say, what I do, and who I am. That's why I argue that the most important preparation the communicator makes is the spiritual preparation. What you say counts, but not as much as what you do. And what you do is important, but not as important as who you are.

Looking back over my years as a student in Sunday schools, I realize the teachers who made the big difference in my life were people who really knew God in a powerful way. They weren't the most gifted verbally, and visually there were some things they did that weren't up to the standard of perfection I set. But there was something about them that made me know they knew this Jesus they were telling me about. Jesus Christ was somebody special to them and that made them special to me.

The Personification Principle

The personification principle is exciting. To think God wrapped up the idea of grace in His Son and sent Him to planet earth is awesome. Then, to realize this Jesus has moved into the lives of those who love Him, and through them is making that amazing idea known to other men, is thrilling! When you grab hold of the truth that you are one of the persons that idea has been wrapped up in—that's wonderfully powerful!

4

Directives to Disciplers

Your Majesty,
Some men's ambition is art,
Some men's ambition is fame,
Some men's ambition is gold,
My ambition is the souls of men.
General William Booth

And Jesus came and spake unto them, saying, All power is given unto me in heaven and in earth. Go ye therefore, and teach all nations, baptizing them in the name of the Father, and of the Son, and of the Holy Ghost: teaching them to observe all things whatsoever I have commanded you: and, lo, I am with you alway, even unto the end of the world. Amen.

Matthew 28:18-20

A country preacher was asked his opinion of the sermon he had just heard an eloquent minister deliver. With characteristic kindness and honesty, he responded, "Well, the brother did a mighty fine job with the big idea, but he needs to learn how to specificate."

I've felt the same way many times when I've been trapped in the captive audience of someone who has a great idea, but doesn't seem to know how to put wheels on it. I want to stand up and say, "I vote yes on your proposal. Now tell me how to help it happen. 'Specificate' please."

That criticism can't be leveled against Jesus when

He talked about discipleship and discipling. He was very detailed in His directive and told the disciples what they were to do, how they were to do it, and how to know when the job had been done. His explicit directions are contained in the Great Commission portion of Matthew's Gospel.

Three Words to Build a Ministry On

The last few verses of Matthew 28 have long been popular with preachers. From the many sermons you have heard taken from this text, you may have concluded the big word in this passage is *go*. I can easily understand how you might have come to that conclusion because it seems most sermons start and stop with that word.

I don't deny we must move out of our own little world and become missionaries to the world around us, if we are to be obedient to the command of Christ. But I will argue that Jesus did not raise His voice when He said, "Go." He saved His emphasis for the word we translate *teach*. In fact, a better way of saying what Jesus said in the original is, "As you are going, make disciples."

Jesus knew the "go" was built into the "gospel" and His men would be movers. They would either be drawn to distant places and people by the desire to share the good news with them or driven to their posts of discipling duty by the persecution that was inevitable. The Lord was giving direction concerning what they were to do as they went with the Word. So He gave them three words—*teach, teaching, observe.* These told them what they were to do, how they were to do it, and how to know when their mission was accomplished. Those words are *(matheteuo)* teach; *(didasko)* teaching; and *(tereo)* observe. Let's take a closer look at them.

Teach

Teach is the big word because it declares the grand goal of disciplers. It does more than describe one of the things we are to do; it states the total task and makes us know evangelism is our reason for being.

Matheteuo is the original word and I think it is best translated "disciple." That's because "teach" has a classroom connotation in the minds of most of us and our mental image doesn't match the massive implications of the word. It is a word big enough to describe evangelistic crusades, missionary ministries, and the total task of the local church. It is a word that declares evangelism to be the *what* of our calling. The best way I know to say to you what it says to me is, "Communicate Christ!"

In chapter 3, we thought about the process of communication so I won't talk more about this concept. I'll just remind you we are called to "pass on" the life of the Lord Jesus Christ to those around us. That's the command contained in the word *matheteuo* and, any way you translate it, the meaning is evangelism.

Sunday schools have always been at their best when their purpose was plainly evangelistic. When the noble purpose of saving the soul of the student gives way to just educating the mind and clothing and feeding the body, the momentum is lost and the effort eventually falters and fails. When a man's heart quits, he dies. And when the heart of the church—a passion for souls—dies, it doesn't take the organization long to collapse.

The successful Sunday schools of our day are those where the leadership is committed to the Sunday school as a strategy for saving souls. The ones in trouble are seemingly searching for a purpose and the only thing that keeps them going is the empty shell of a tradition that demands a Sunday school hour before church each Lord's Day.

I have observed two approaches to evangelism through the Sunday school. For want of better terms, I have tagged them "direct" and "indirect" and have watched them both produce remarkable results. They may be blended into an integrated strategy in a church or a church may opt for the exclusive use of one or the other. I am personally more comfortable with the mix of the two, but I argue for no set style. The only thing I insist on is that a Sunday school be committed to a strategy of evangelism.

The Direct Approach

I grew up in a church in Pratt, Kansas, and I still remember going with my pastor father to work on the Sunday school bus and riding with him when he drove it. It wasn't much of a bus, but then Pratt wasn't much of a town, and it covered the territory well enough. At least it did until one day it stalled on the railroad tracks and a passing train put it out of commission. Of course, that didn't stop us. We just found another way to "go out and get them" for Jesus.

That direct-evangelism strategy worked well in that time and place. True, it was primarily preacher-centered and our services were much more evangelistic in style. But the sinners came, listened, and walked the aisle to get saved. And there are still many places where this strategy is working.

The Indirect Approach

Several years since then, I find myself pastoring a church in Santa Ana, California, and I must admit things have changed a bit. In the middle of tract houses, crowded freeways, and frantic folk, the old strategies have had to give way to a different emphasis. No, I haven't given up on evangelism. Actually, I believe it is our only reason for being. But I have had to face the fact that, for us, evangelism is more indirect than direct and our major effort is given to the "perfecting [equipping] of the saints, for the work of the ministry" (Ephesians 4:12).

This doesn't mean we don't call people to Christ in our public services. We do! But we also place a great emphasis on ministering to those who minister, and it is exciting to see the ministry of the church being multiplied as the members become the evangelists who penetrate their parish.

Sunday school is a major part of our effort to build the congregation up in their faith and train them in the techniques of giving it away. I suppose we will always struggle to get the level of involvement we want in this task, but for those who share our burden for evangelism, we rejoice. And so do they when souls are saved.

The style may be direct or indirect, but the strategy is the same. We are proclaiming the good news and calling people to follow Jesus Christ. Evangelism must be our passion if we are to be true to the real Sunday school spirit. Robert Raikes was motivated by his passion to evangelize through education, as was another great change agent, General William Booth. He exhorted his followers, "Go for souls, and go for the worst." King Edward VII called him to Buckingham Palace in 1904 and told him, "You are doing a good work; a great work, General Booth." Before leaving the palace, he was asked to write in the king's autograph book. Taking pen in hand, the 75-year-old Booth wrote:

> Your Majesty,
> Some men's ambition is art,
> Some men's ambition is fame,
> Some men's ambition is gold,
> My ambition is the souls of men.

The Pittsburgh Steelers were the winners of the 1979 Super Bowl. After it was over, a reporter mentioned their slogan, which I think explained their success. In just three little words they said it all and explained the difference between winners and losers. The three words? "Whatever it takes!"

That is the way we must feel about obedience to the command of Christ to communicate. Discipling is demanded by the Great Commission. We have no choice but to obey and that means we must do whatever it takes. And what it takes is teaching.

Teaching

The word translated *teaching* in the King James Version is *didasko* and suggests the purposeful and persistent presentation of truth. It means to give instruction and reminds us of God's great plan for presenting His love to man. The God of glory was the Great Instructor when He spoke to mankind using the Word which became flesh and dwelt among us. That Word was Jesus and He was faithful to follow His Father's example as He gave instruction to those who would hear Him. He so faithfully followed His Father's formula, He became famous as the Great Teacher.

Jesus was also a miracle worker and healer, but His transformation of the Twelve and others is directly traced to His teachings. By His demonstrations of power, He got their attention, but it was through the truth He taught them that they came to understand who they were and their relationship with their Heavenly Father.

When He sent His disciples out to disciple, He told them to do as He had done and He used the term *teaching*. The word *matheteuo* tells us what to do and the word *didasko* (teaching) tells us how it is done.

John Garlock, in his book *Teaching as Jesus Taught* (Springfield, MO: Gospel Publishing House, 1966), defines preaching as: "The proclamation of the living word (Jesus) through the written word (Scripture) by the spoken word (Utterance of the Teacher)." I like this definition because it traces how truth in the form and force of Jesus Christ is transmitted to the student. To be privileged to be a participant in this process is exciting and every Sunday school teacher should count himself blessed to be a communicator of Christ.

Obviously, there is more to teaching than 1 hour on Sunday morning. In fact, the world is our classroom and everything that happens to us plays a part in our education through experience. The total church and family-life experience are involved in the religious education of our children. It is not fair to push a child into a classroom and expect a teacher to do all there is to do in just 60 minutes on Sunday morning. This is not to downplay the importance of ministries of formalized instruction. I am just saying that for a child to have the best chance possible of getting to know God in a life-changing way, there must be a total team effort involving the church and family.

Of course, the Holy Spirit often compensates for our inadequacies and makes up for our mistakes. Many wonderful changes in lives have happened in spite of, instead of because of, the church and home. But this doesn't give us an excuse to take lightly our responsibility when it comes to teaching.

As a student of growing churches, I have isolated two factors that are evident in all those where real growth is taking place. Before I mention the factors, I suppose I should define "real growth." By "real growth" I mean growth that is solid and steady, not based on a "hype" approach or personality parade. I mean the sort of growth that is evidenced in attendance and offering figures and in the life change of the members. That sort of total growth is evident in several churches I've studied and what they all have in common is an emphasis on the Word of God and the worship of God.

The pastors of these churches take seriously their responsibility as pastor/teacher and the people are responding with excitement to truth being taught. Add to this a growing awareness in the charismatic renewal of the need for solid Biblical instruction and the rediscovery that teaching in the home is absolutely required if the Christian home is to survive, and you have a new ground swell of excitement regarding the ministry of teaching.

Recently developed strategies for training teachers by denominations and publishing houses have impacted on the church and we are better for them. I can only say thank God for them and wish they had been developed sooner.

A report I read recently makes me wonder about the seriousness of some of the efforts the church has put forth in this vital area. According to the report, 150 college freshmen were given a Bible knowledge test and some of the worst answers included these misstatements:

"The story of Abraham is found in the Book of Ruth. Joan of Arc was the Hebrew heroine who saved her people from the hatred of Haman. Exodus involved the return of the Jews to Palestine after WW II. The Wisdom Books of the Bible are Acts, Paradise Lost, and Lord of the Flies."

The answers are even more disturbing when you consider that the average test taker had approximately 1,500 hours of Sunday school behind him. Of course, most answers weren't that bad, but the overall test scores were bad enough to give some credence to *Life* magazine's controversial description of Sunday school as the most wasted hour in the week.

Obviously, we can and must do better. There is more at stake here than correct answers on a Bible knowledge test. We are really talking about lives that need changing. Biblical ignorance is bound to show up in behavior patterns. That is why we must make a commitment to quality teaching and Sunday schools. Lives need transforming and that will only happen when we teach for life change.

Observe

The last of the three big words recorded in Matthew's statement of the Great Commission is the word *observe*. It means more than seeing; it suggests doing.

Let me illustrate it this way. Imagine me driving to my office one morning and pulling off the road and parking in front of a 55-mph speed sign. Now that I've parked, I just sit and stare at the sign until a California Highway Patrol car stops and the officer asks what is happening. Then, with my most innocent smile, I explain, "I'm observing the speed limit."

Now what do you think would happen? You'd probably say he would suspect I was crazy and without delay he would hustle me off to the nearest funny farm. Why? Because when the law says "observe the speed limit," it doesn't mean for me to park and stare at a sign. It means for me to drive 55 mph.

I believe you understand that when Matthew used the word *observe* he was suggesting something far beyond the idea of just looking at the life offered by Jesus. He didn't mean for us to just look at it; He meant for us to live it, abundantly.

Henrietta Mears liked to remind teachers that a "teacher has not taught until a learner has learned." I would agree with her and add that when a learner really learns it will make a difference in his life. His behavior will witness more loudly than any words he might speak. It is what he does after he says he believes that is the true test of the truth's impact on him.

In the next chapter, I'll have more to say about teach-

ing that effects life change and the levels of learning a
student must be moved through before a teacher can
say, "Mission accomplished." For now, suffice it to say
there is a great distance between rote learning, the
lowest rung on the ladder, and the realization level
where the learner demonstrates mastery and ownership of the idea by doing what he has discovered. Jesus
was speaking of this ultimate level of learning when
He promised, "Ye shall know the truth, and the truth
shall make you free" (John 8:32). The same thing is
suggested by James in his exhortation to be "doers of
the word, and not hearers only" (James 1:22).

The teacher must never assume his responsibility
ends with the first telling of the truth. It may take many
times of telling until the life of the learner shows he has
received and now owns the idea. One idea wrapped up
in the word *teaching (didasko)* is repetition. It is a
tremendous teaching tool and we as teachers must remember to keep on teaching a truth until a learner
gives evidence of having learned it by obvious life
change.

The other day I heard a not-so-true story about a
preacher who candidated for and then was called to a
pastorate. To his congregation's surprise, he repeated
his try-out sermon on his first official Sunday as pastor.
But even worse, he kept repeating it Sunday after Sunday until the board of deacons held a special meeting to
call attention to and resolve the problem. When the
spokesman asked the pastor if he realized he had been
repeating the same sermon each week, the pastor said,
"Of course, I do." The deacon then asked, "Don't you
have any other sermons?" Once again the preacher
responded, "Of course, I do." "Then why don't you use
them?" the deacon challenged. Looking the deacon
right in the eye, the preacher said, "Just as soon as I see
evidence that you people are getting the point of this
one, I'll move on to sermon number two."

Smile if you will at this story, but don't overlook the important point it makes. It is time we took seriously our responsibility to teach and preach for life change and refuse to be satisfied with any other response.

Jesus wasn't joking when He said we were to teach (evangelize) through teaching (education) until those taught have learned to observe (obey or do) those things He taught them. They were told to go out and teach for life change and that's just what they did. They became famous for turning the world right side up and we are their descendants and disciples. What they were called to begin, we have been called to continue.

To be obedient to the command of Christ, I think we must believe three things and then do one thing. First, we must believe things and people aren't right and the world needs changing. Then, we must grasp the truth that Jesus Christ is the great change Agent and He can and will make an eternal difference in those who come to know Him. Last, we must believe He has called us to know Him and make Him known. Having come to that certain knowledge, we must live what we teach by doing what we have discovered.

5
Teaching for Life Change

Conversion: act of converting.
Convert: change; turn; change from unbelief to faith.
Thorndike Barnhouse Comprehensive
Desk Dictionary

Therefore if any man be in Christ, he is a new creature: old things are passed away; behold, all things are become new.

2 Corinthians 5:17

"What do you think of all this talk about behavioral objectives?" The question came from a seminarian in the group that had gathered around me following a motivational message I had just delivered to a meeting of Christian educators. Waiting for my ride to the hotel, I had been enjoying the small talk with my new friends. Then came the verbal bomb—"behavioral objectives."

I think he was testing my level of knowledge in the field and trying to find out just how much of an expert I was. He had been introduced to the concept in his classes, and fortunately I had heard about the idea from one of my divisional directors who happened to be a public school administrator as well as a Sunday school enthusiast. She had given me a good introduction to the system of judging learning on the basis of behavior and we had even held some training sessions for our teaching teams which introduced and

emphasized the idea. So when he dropped the bomb-
shell, my foxhole had been dug and I was ready to respond confidently, "I'm glad you asked that question." (If only I could always be that lucky!)

It only took me a minute to let him know I knew
something about the new terminology. Then I was able
to remind us all the idea isn't really new. Jesus understood behavioral objectives. That's why He told His
disciples to evaluate their teaching in terms of observ-
able behavior changes. Remember that last big word in
chapter 4? It was *tereo;* it is translated "observe" and
means "do." *The Living Bible, Today's English
Version,* and the popular *New International Version*
use the word *obey* in place of the word *observe* to
help us understand truth is to be translated into life
change. The new attitude is to produce new actions;
those who were rebellious toward God begin to become obedient children of the heavenly household.

We are aiming to produce change as the result of the
proclamation of the gospel. The idea is suggested by
our religious terminology. We call for conversion
(change) and those who respond in belief are called
converts. By this we mean the convert has moved
from unbelief to belief and a new life in Christ. Paul
explained it this way to the Corinthians in his second
letter to them: "Therefore if any man be in Christ, he
is a new creature: old things are passed away; behold,
all things are become new" (2 Corinthians 5:17).

We understand that to "know the Lord" is to be
changed by that knowledge. And we also know, but
sometimes don't seem to understand, this knowledge
of the Lord involves much more than an intellectual
understanding. But how do you know when someone
really knows the Lord? You answer, "You can tell by
the change." And I agree.

We say we can tell when someone comes to really
know the Lord by the changed life he begins to live.

That's true, but do we know how a person moves from the beginning point of an awareness of the possibility of new life in Jesus Christ to the actual experience of living that life? Because I think it is important for change agents like Sunday school teachers and other Christian communicators to understand the mechanics of the process, look with me at the five levels of learning: repeat, recognize, realize, relate, and reproduce.

Levels of Learning

At the beginning only the teacher owns the idea to be communicated. Then, the idea is coded into a word and sent to and received by the student. He may go so far as to repeat the word after the teacher at this level but it holds little value for him. The teacher then explains the unknown word in known terms. A definition of the word is given and the student begins to understand it as he steps up to the rung of recognition. Level three is reached as the teacher leads the student to discover the concept is Biblical and the idea is part of God's plan for His people.

On level four, the transfer of ownership from teacher to student begins to be noticeable. Like the passing of the baton in a relay race, the idea is moved into the hand of the learner as he begins to relate ancient truth to contemporary times. He begins to realize the people of the Bible have much in common with him and their response to God provides both positive and negative patterns that give direction for life today. Finally, on level five the student has decided to take personal possession of the truth and he begins to reproduce it in his own life.

Now let's go through the process just described and do a thing we used to call "play-like" when I was a kid. Let's "play-like" I'm the teacher and you are the student and the truth I want to teach you is the one wrapped up in the word *hallelujah*. Play-like you've never heard it before. We are in Sunday school and the teacher (me) has just walked into the room.

"Good morning, students," I begin. Then I say, "Today I am going to introduce you to a powerful word that will change your life." (Now let's watch the process unfold on a paragraph-by-paragraph basis.)

Repeat (The ability to say words without knowledge of meaning.)

"That word is *hallelujah*." Then I repeat it and ask you to say it after me. Now you have taken the first step. A word has been spoken in your hearing and you have mastered it; at least on the rote level. But the fact you can say the word doesn't mean you know what it means. So, I proceed to step two.

Recognize (The ability to recognize the meaning of a word when it is heard.)

"It means 'Praise Jehovah' or 'Praise the Lord,' " I explain. I go on to give you a working definition of the word so when you hear it you will understand, at least intellectually, what a speaker is saying when he uses that term.

Realize (The ability to recognize the concept in a Biblical setting and as a part of the divine design.)

"Now tell me someone you have read about in the Bible who said hallelujah a lot," I challenge. And because you are so bright, you quickly answer, "David." Now we have a model that helps us understand the concept in real-life terms and we realize it is proper for the people of God to give Him praise. But we still aren't home free. You may buy the idea that David did it and it was good for him, but fail to understand its relevance to you today. After all, what else did David have to do but watch a few sheep, play his harp on a grassy hillside, and say "hallelujah" now and then? What place does that word have in the vocabulary of a hassled, harried human trying to survive in the 20th century?

Relate (The ability to relate a timeless idea to your present experience and recognize its relevance.)

"Let's talk about the relevance of that word *hallelujah* and the power of praise and what it means to us," I now urge. And a spirited showing of opinions begins. In the process, you talk about your problems and others do the same and together you recognize the need for power in your life. Then someone shares how he has been helped by praising the Lord and you become convinced it's a good idea to say "hallelujah." About then the bell rings, the class ends, and you are out the door with the others; leaving me to pat myself on the back for a job well done.

But it isn't finished yet. Oh yes, class is over and I've done all I can. But the mission isn't accomplished until we meet on the street a few days later and you excitedly say, "Praise the Lord! I'm glad to see you because I've got something exciting to tell you. The Lord just did something great for me and I'm praising Him for it."

Reproduce (The ownership of the idea and the actualizing of the concept in a way that reproduces it.)

While you tell me the exciting experience that made you say, "Praise the Lord," I rejoice in it and in the fact you have been grabbed by the gratitude attitude and discovered the pleasure and power of praise. Although you may not use the exact word *hallelujah,* you say it in your own way and the idea is now being reproduced by your life. At first it was my idea, but now you own it too. You've gotten the idea and the idea has gotten you. Hallelujah!

You can work through this same process using any word you want. Of course, the presentation will vary in style but the basic idea will stay the same. Jesus Christ himself is communicated in this way. At first He may be just a name, but in the final understanding He is a powerful Presence within. The task of the teacher is to continue to communicate until Christ is known on the ultimate level and His life becomes evident through the life of the student. When that happens, you have a convert and that means he's been changed for time and eternity.

Teaching for Life Change

Learning is change and change is learning. That oft-repeated truism must be understood by every teacher. We teach to change people from death to life and the way this is done is by teaching them Jesus Christ. In that beautiful invitation of Jesus to all that "labor and are heavy laden," we hear the Saviour say: "Take my yoke upon you, and learn of me; for I am meek and lowly in heart: and ye shall find rest unto your souls" (Matthew 11:29). Note that "learn of me" phrase. It's the secret to life change. Jesus also declared himself to be the "truth" in His three-part description of himself recorded in John 14:6, and we know from what He taught us that to know the truth is to be set free.

The challenge is to communicate Christ in a way that moves Him through our life into other lives and liberates them from the power of sin. Now let's look at a three-stage strategy for doing just that.

Know, Feel, Do

These words are printed on the "teaching/learning aim plan sheet" we use to introduce teachers to lesson planning. They help the teacher target three vital parts of the student's experience and guide in the preparation of a presentation that will produce the desired results. The word *know* is a cognitive goal and deals with what the student must know and the information he must possess to make the proper decision. *Feel* is the word we use to identify the affective goal or the way the student must feel to respond properly. *Do* is the word we use to define the desired behavior or the acceptable response.

These are not only good words to guide us in our planning, they also describe the way a student learns and how the change called learning occurs.

Usually you begin at the beginning—right? Wrong! You must first take the time to target. Before you take the first step toward a goal, you must define that goal. That's why we teach teachers to prayerfully visualize the result they desire and then begin to take the necessary steps to make it happen. For example, an unconverted student needs to be born again. Get that goal fixed firmly in mind and begin to pray and proceed toward it. The public confession of faith by that student is your behavioral objective.

Now you must deal with the question: "How must the student feel to make a commitment of his life to Christ?" To those who would argue that feelings don't count, I would respectfully reply, "You don't know what you are talking about." Scientists who have studied the human personality tell us the major decisions of our lives are not made with our heads but with our hearts. The wife we marry, the kind of car we drive, and many other decisions we make are intellectual only to a point. It's our emotional man who makes the choice and our feelings are the force that motivates us. This means you must understand that the student you want to see saved must feel warmly welcomed by a God of love who has reached out to him through His suffering Son, Jesus Christ.

That should clarify the *know* goal. Because you know what you want the student to do—accept Christ as his personal Saviour—and you know how he must feel before he will do what you want him to do, you should now know what he needs to know. He obviously needs to know Jesus Christ gave His life for him as a demonstration of divine love. He needs to know that all he must do is receive by faith the fact of God's grace. So that's what you tell him. You tell him and tell him and keep on telling him until he hears you, and in hearing you finds himself drawn by the loving voice of God's Spirit.

It works this way. First, we have to know something on the cognitive level. Then it affects us on the affective or emotional level. Finally, our feelings trigger an action response and in that moment we know by experiment and experience the idea presented is true. Many times our learning experiences in the world end up as disappointments, but at least we learn what's not right and in the process move one step closer to finding out what is right. But Jesus Christ is always right, always truth. When we present Him to a pupil, there is never disappointment when that student steps out in faith and actualizes his trust in Jesus Christ, Son of God and Saviour.

A few years ago, my son Stephen went skiing for the first time. Before heading for the top of the mountain that morning, my wife and I turned him over to the ski instructor. When his lesson ended, we met him at the ski school and shared his pride in the progress he had made. The instructor told us he was a natural athlete—something every father likes to hear about his boy—and he suggested I take him up for a run down the lower slope.

So up we went. He was excited to show me what he had learned and the first part of the run was fun as I watched him move straight down the slope under control. He wasn't moving too fast and I was able to slide backwards to keep between him and other skiers. But before long, I had to tell him to turn right to miss some trouble ahead. When he kept skiing straight, I told him again and this time he told me he couldn't.

"But I thought you told me he taught you to turn," I said. And he answered, "He did!" "So turn right like he taught you," I urged. That's when he said something I'll never forget. With a look of doom on his face he shouted, "He taught me but I didn't learn!" A moment later he went down in a heap.

Of course, he got back up and after putting his skis back on and adjusting his bindings, we headed for the lodge. This time, I had him cradled between my knees and as we skied down he matched my moves and began again the process of learning how to turn.

As a teacher of truth, I must teach and teach and teach until the learner has really learned. How will I know when that happens? When the message has been mastered it will show in the life. What the student knows and feels will eventually be demonstrated in what he does.

This ends the theory segment of this book. So I want to talk briefly about the proverbial "bottom line." Life change is the first and last line of the Sunday school spirit story. Jesus Christ came to change lives and He did. The world still needs changing and Jesus still

changes people for time and eternity. So let's get on with the task of communicating Christ. Let's transform through teaching. By so doing, we will be true to the Sunday school spirit.

6
Who Needs It?

The holiest moment of the church service is the moment when God's people, strengthened by preaching and sacrament, go out of the church door into the world to be the Church. We don't go to church; we are the Church.

Ernest Southcott

And I say also unto thee, That thou art Peter, and upon this rock I will build my church; and the gates of hell shall not prevail against it.

Matthew 16:18

When is gospel music not gospel music? Answer: When it says something stupid like, "Me and Jesus got our own thing goin', we don't need nobody to tell us what it's all about."

If you haven't heard that line before, consider yourself blessed and then pray for those who have heard it and started singing along. Unfortunately, it expresses an attitude that is all too evident in Christianity today. And a lot of unthinking believers are buying the idea of saying "yes" to Christ, but "no" to community. To those of us who urge them to commit themselves to a body of believers they reply, "The church—who needs it?"

In this day of mass-media ministry, we are witnessing a remarkable response to electronic evangelism. But we are also aware of a follow-up gap that is alarming. A recent major evangelism effort that utilized radio, TV, bumper stickers, lapel pins, billboards, and telephone contacts was so successful a survey showed two-thirds of the population in a given area was aware of it. And the number of "decisions for Christ" was most encouraging. But in the final analysis, only 3 percent of those who made decisions for Christ became church members. While rejoicing in the 3 percent, I must still ask, "What went wrong?"

I suppose there are three possible "whipping boys" before us. We can blame the media ministry, the so-called converts, or the church.

Perhaps the problem is the presentation. The slick, neatly packaged salvation show may be guilty of presenting the delights of "deciding for Christ" without the demands of discipleship. Could it be the gospel the electronic church is communicating is, as some detractors declare, a shallow substitute for the Cross-centered discipleship that should be demanded? That's a hard question that must eventually be answered by every preacher, regardless of the pulpit he preaches from.

There are some who would argue that the problem isn't the presentation, but the type of people who repond. They tell us people are generally shallow and emotional in their response and have always been like that. They point persuasively to the 5,000 who ate the bread and fish as compared to the 12 that walked with Jesus. There is no question, the church has a tough task. We are called to minister to a world that is so confused it is trying to war its way to peace, spend its way to wealth, and enjoy its way to heaven. Those who offer an easy way—who preach a materialistic message of "all this and heaven too"—are bound to have remarkable results. But how real are these confessions of faith? Have they produced converts?

The third possible culprit is the church itself. It has

been argued that the church is content to close itself inside its sanctuaries while the rest of the world goes to hell. The comfortable pew is constantly condemned, but even in churches that call themselves evangelical there is too often a tendency to be bothered by outsiders who take insiders' pews. Many pastors find themselves frustrated by the failure of members to extend themselves toward the unchurched with evangelistic enthusiasm.

Obviously, there are no easy answers. I believe the blame must be shared by all of us and we must all restate a belief in the church of Jesus Christ as the supreme strategy of the Spirit in this day and time.

Jesus Christ declared himself dramatically when He told Simon Peter: "I will build my church; and the gates of hell shall not prevail against it" (Matthew 16: 18). Paul the apostle wrote to the Ephesians about a Christ who "loved the church, and gave himself for it" (Ephesians 5:25). When you understand the Church has become the very body of Christ, then it is obvious that the answer to the question, "Who needs the church?" is, "Christ does." For it is through His church that He is living out His life in the world today.

Another obvious answer to the question is, "The world does." Except for the salvation purchased by the breaking of the physical body of Christ and now proclaimed by the mystical body of Christ, there is no hope for lost humanity. Without the body of Christ, we face the eternal damnation of hell. But, because of what Christ has done, we are offered the eternal delight of heaven.

Beyond the obvious answers just offered, it should be noted that we as individual members of the church of Christ need the other members—the total body of Christ—if we are to be complete. The Lone Ranger type Christian is missing the point and the privileges that are his if he disregards the admonition in Hebrews to forsake not "the assembling of ourselves together, as the manner of some is" (10:25). It is in this community, this fellowship of the forgiven, that we find our purpose and develop our gifts. While it is not the function of the organized church to create a changed society, it is the function of the community of Christians to create the creators of a changed society.

The Church Defined

To converse about the church can be confusing unless you are clear on your definition. The word *church* may be used to describe the mystical body of Christ comprised of all those who have placed their faith in Him. It can also be used to describe a building used by worshipers or the service they hold in it. A local organized body of believers may be called a church; as may a worldwide fellowship of such local churches.

My primary emphasis from this point forward will be the local body of believers called a church. My definition is in the interest of zeroing in on the techniques of our task as evangelists and it reflects my basic bias as the pastor of a local church. Frankly, I believe congregations like the one I'm privileged to pastor are the bricks God is using to build the great House of faith. Statistics cited by high-profile ministries may be impressive when compared to one local church's results, but when you combine it with all the other Christ-honoring churches in the community, county, state, nation, and world—well, I think you see my point. The local church will never be replaced by parachurch ministries no matter how glamorous they appear. God is to be praised for the miracles of media ministries that have raised the consciousness of our communities concerning Christ, but thank God too for your local church and the privilege of being part of a ministry that offers deciders for Christ an opportunity to become disciples.

The Church is an organism, an organization, and an event. I would gladly give credit to the person who said that sentence first but, for the life of me, I can't remember where I read this definition of the church. It is a succinct statement that captures the concept communicated by the word *church*. The words *organism*, *organization*, and *event* provide a triangle of truth that should remind you of the fellowship you function in and through.

First, the local church is a living entity comprised of those who have passed from death to life through faith in Jesus Christ. Those who were dead in trespasses and sins have been resurrected, born again, to newness of life. This is the secret of the church; the dynamic difference that separates it from other civic and social organizations. It is not an organization for the sake of organization. It is a living entity, a force that expresses itself in the form of organization. The difference between a true church and a civic club is much like the difference between a real live human being and a figure in the Hollywood Wax Museum. When Jesus Christ is alive in the hearts of believers, you have a living body, an *organism*. And if you don't first have that, you really have nothing at all.

This organism is expressed in *organization*. The word becomes flesh; the life of Christ becomes a body of believers, and a community is created. There are some who dislike organization, thinking it unspiritual. Their favorite Bible verse seems to be the one about "having a form of godliness, but denying the power thereof" (2 Timothy 3:5). They don't seem to realize that verse is only a call for balance. It isn't an argument against form. An organism must have an organization through which to express its power and purpose.

So the organized church becomes a vehicle for doing what the spirit of life within motivates it to do.

The last word in the definition is *event*. It describes what happens when the organism expresses itself through an organization. Event is what happens when the members of the church come together to celebrate their faith and call others to experience new life in Christ. It is what happens when a Sunday school is organized and the church is called to commitment, or when the church moves outside the sanctuary to confront the world around it with the claims of Christ.

An Event or Events

Unfortunately, some churchmen fail to "see the forest for the trees." They tend to think in compartments; separating the varied strategies of the church and making a difference between the departments. When this happens, there are problems produced by the competition that is inevitable.

We must learn to think of the church and its ministries as a single unit. Like the old song suggests, "Like a mighty army moves the church of God." Sure, there are units within the unit—various parts of the body— but all units and parts must be blended together into a single entity lest we destroy our effectiveness by our divisions.

The music, missions, preaching, and teaching ministries are to be united in purpose and pointed toward the same goal.

Sunday School and Church

I would argue at this point for *integration*. Especially as it relates to the blending of Sunday school and church. As a former minister of Christian education and now a pastor, I am completely convinced they go together like the proverbial horse and carriage. Robert

Raikes was a churchman before he was a Sunday school enthusiast. And the Sunday school system has proved to be one of the best strategies for soul winning—the work of the church.

I remember filling out my Crown Record System tally sheet on Sundays as a kid and proudly noting I had brought my Bible and planned to stay for church. In those days, we usually had more in Sunday school than in the worship hour. But now the trend seems to be just the opposite. Frankly, I don't like either extreme. I believe in balance and I don't think you can beat the dynamic duo of Sunday school and church.

The Sunday school classroom is a great place to introduce ideas and lay the factual foundations for the experiences the student will be encouraged to enter into in the worship service. The worship service and other aspects of the church experience become the laboratory for testing ideas introduced in the classroom.

Two noteworthy areas in which there must be a balance between theory and practice are worship and works. You can talk all you want about these ideas in the classroom, but eventually they must be dealt with on an experimental basis, and the church becomes the laboratory.

Learning to Worship God

Take, for example, our worship. It is important for the student to be given a theoretical framework. But then there must come the experience of walking into the presence of God and knowing Him in the worship experience.

There is a great deal of teaching and learning involved in valid worship. As logs must be properly placed before the fire is set in a fireplace, so there are truths that must be put in place before the fire of God's presence burns brightly. A worship experience that is lit on logs of truth tends to flare brightly for a few moments, then burn down to cold ashes. A better way to worship is to make proper preparation before the worship begins, then as the fire burns, continue to add the fuel of Biblical knowledge to the flame of spiritual presence.

There are few things I enjoy more than a snowy day in a mountain cabin with a crackling fire in the fireplace. I really enjoy tending the fire. It is therapy to me that is hard to explain. I minister to that fire by adding the logs needed to keep it going and it ministers back to me with the beauty of its blaze. I feel the same way about spiritual worship. I must bring to the experience the logs of learning that the Spirit of God can ignite and then set the fire that gives the glorious glow that proves His presence.

In my study of growing churches today, I have discovered in each a blend of the Word of God being faithfully taught and the worship of God being fervently experienced. It is apparent to me that learning about worship in our Sunday schools and through our sermons is only completed by learning to worship in our times of prayer and praise. It is an ongoing experience and requires a church to make a place for both the teaching of truth about worship and the testing of that truth in the laboratory of experience.

Because we believe in this balance we guard carefully the right of our people to enjoy an uninterrupted Sunday school session and we also urge parents to bring their children to the sanctuary services. Extended sessions are provided for only preschool through grade two during our morning worship hours. The older children worship with their parents. Some suggest the children don't understand all that is happening. This is true of all of us who witness the miraculous ministry of the Holy Spirit through a worship service. But children and adults do sense something special when God makes His presence known in our midst. And as the parents and other people around the child worship, he is able to begin to model their methods and share their experiences.

Comments made by our children to their parents about sermons and other parts of the services are heartwarming and confirm our contention that there is more to church for them than Sunday school. Sunday school is a vital part of the process of learning, but so is the opportunity to experience worship. That is why we believe in a balanced, well-integrated strategy.

Looking at it from the other direction, I think it is just as important that adults take time for church and Sunday school. Unfortunately, some adults have the silly idea that Sunday school is just for kids. Nonsense! I urge all our people to participate in a weekly class experience because it's in this environment that questions and answers can produce a greater understanding of who God is, and the worship experience is inevitably enhanced.

As growing churches expand in size, it often becomes necessary to move to multiple services. Unfortunately, some leaders decide Sunday school for adults isn't as important as the worship services and they plan schedules that reflect this feeling and frustrate the adult Sunday school student. I always argue against this because the opportunity to participate in Bible study and worship should be the inalienable right of every member regardless of age.

Remember, balance is beautiful. It is in the Sunday school we learn the principles of worship and it is in the sanctuary service we put into practice those principles. If our churches are to produce people who know God and are able to worship Him in Spirit and in truth, we must take seriously the concept of integrated ministries for a common goal—the glory of God.

Learning to Work

Much of what I have just said about worship, the mystical side of our experience, is also true concerning the practical side of worship or stewardship. The church must teach by word and example that there is more to worship than hymns, prayer, and praise.

Ernest Southcott, writing in the *Christian Herald,* said it this way: "The holiest moment of the church service is the moment when God's people, strengthened by preaching and sacrament, go out of the church door into the world to be the Church. We don't go to church; we are the Church."

Paul urged the Romans to offer their bodies as living sacrifices and argued that this was but an expression of reasonable service and spiritual worship. And who isn't aware of the strong position taken by James regarding the importance of proving faith by works? It should be clear to all that valid worship will produce vital works and it is the mission of the church to prepare people for a life of stewardship.

Like mystical worship, stewardship is something that must be taught in the classroom and then tested in the laboratory of life. A balanced and integrated ministry will offer people both opportunities. Children and adults deserve the privilege of discovering the discipline aspects of discipleship in and through the church experience.

The good thing about joining a church and making a promise to participate is the new member is faced with the responsibilities that come with that privilege. I think we owe it to our people to constantly keep before them these obligations and give them adequate teaching concerning stewardship of time, talents, and treasury; then offer them ample opportunities for responding to that teaching. This can be done through offerings, service opportunities, and the use of God-given gifts.

The last part of Acts 2 describes the Early Church and states three important things about that fellowship of the forgiven. According to verse 42, they gathered together around "the apostle's doctrine." They also united themselves in loving unity and fellowship. The third factor, evangelism, is evident as you read verses 43 through 47. Because of their faithfulness to God's truth and one another, they possessed spiritual power that was awesome. And the natural result was the growth of that body on a daily basis.

To those who might have asked in those days, "Who needs the church?" I think the answer would have been: *Christ needs the Church* to manifest His love and power through. It is His body formed for that purpose. The individual members of the church need the church for teaching, training, and spiritual support in the ministry given to each member. And the lost, confused world needs the church. It is the only hope of society.

The world still needs the church today. Those answers remain valid. But what sort of church does it need? It needs a church that is balanced in its ministries of education and experience; that mixes the principles of the Word with worship; that is structured and stable, yet spontaneous. I am convinced we can have churches like that today. We desperately need them.

Building a Worshiping, Witnessing, Working Church

A wit once wrote, "When it has all been said and done there is usually more said than done." That can easily be true when it comes to talking about the church. It is a lot easier to write books about building great churches than it is to actually build them.

An anonymous poet spoke the truth when he wrote:

God sends no churches from the skies,
Out of our hearts they must arise.

Jesus Christ, the founder of the Church, paid the ultimate price by laying down His life for it. Those who have followed in His footsteps have sacrificed themselves in building a body of believers through which the living Christ can work His wonders. Whether we are pastors, teachers, or members with many differing gifts, the responsibility still rests on us. We are called to make our contribution to the common goal.

One of the great things about living where I live is I'm privileged to attend major sporting events. When you are there in person, you see things that are missed by the TV audience. For example, at a recent Rose Bowl game, I became very aware of the units within the football team. Perhaps because I was now serving as the senior pastor and directing the ministries of a multiple staff, my attention was attracted to the sideline activities in which the assistant coaches worked with their units.

It was exciting to watch them gather around their leaders for inspiration and instruction before going back on the field to do their thing. It was obvious they shared a common objective with all the other units that made up the team. But they also had specific tasks and were personally responsible for those assignments. As I watched, I realized what a beautiful picture I was seeing of our own local church and the even greater Church, the universal body of believers. We all have the common goal of communicating Christ, but we are each given a specific assignment and made a part of a special team. I left that game having been well entertained and at the same time inspired to work with the church I coach to make it the best it could possibly be.

In my struggle to succeed as a player-coach in the church I serve, I have been guided by a series of questions I think every churchman should ask and answer. I will share them with you and comment on them as a pastor. As you look over my shoulder, I hope you will translate what I've written into truth that fits *you* and *your* ministry. Our positions may vary, but the practical aspects of ministry and the philosophy that guides us should be similar.

What Does the World Need Most?

That's the first question we must ask and answer. A definition of need will make us understand our reason for being. We start by stating that the world needs salvation, the sort of salvation that can come through Jesus Christ alone. He must cancel our guilt and bring order to our lives by becoming our Lord.

When the church starts to settle for secondary goals like social work and civil rights activism, it negates its main mission. The power we possess grows out of an understanding of our purpose.

The world is wrong and needs to be made right. We have become a society of sinners and desperately need salvation. Mankind is rebellious and things have gotten out of control and we need Christ to take charge. In other words, the world needs Jesus. More than anything else, it needs to know the salvation that comes through faith in Him.

What Sort of People Must We Be To Meet That Sort of Need?

Having defined the need of the world to which we must minister, we are now able to understand the sort of people we must be to get the job done. We must be people who *know* and *make known* the Saviour, Jesus Christ. We must be people who communicate

Him constantly by what we say, do, and are. He must live in our lives and show in our contacts with others.

The songwriter prayed, "Let the beauty of Jesus be seen in me." That's the big idea. If the need of the world is to be met we must be a people indwelt by the great need meeter, Jesus Christ.

What Type of Church Produces People Like That?

Having visualized the need and the type of people needed to meet that need, I must now turn my attention to the local church and visualize the sort of church that will produce the kind of people the world needs as witnesses. As I see it, that church must be one in which people are led into a balanced experience of worship and works. This will require the ministries of the church to stress systematic Bible-study opportunities and ample worship opportunities.

I believe a church that will produce a dynamic witness in the world is one in which the leadership understands the creative tension that must exist between the preaching and teaching of the Word of God and worship.

What Type of Leadership Is Needed To Produce That Kind of Church?

Having set priorities, we must then recruit people to help execute these priorities. This principle is applied in my church by having a paid staff and volunteers who serve in the age-level Sunday school classes. Leaders must attract other leaders who will work with them in a team effort that touches every member of the body.

One of the most frustrating things about pastoring a growing church is it seems there is always a part of the fellowship that is just out of reach. That's why I thank the Lord for the principle He modeled when He discipled the Twelve and began His multiplication ministry.

It has been said the leader's greatest ability is his ability to recognize ability. Whatever it is you are called to do, I dare say you need or will soon need help. Now is the time to start prayerfully considering the sort of people God is calling you to call into the ministry.

What Sort of Pastor Produces That Kind of Leadership?

In place of the word *pastor*, I would suggest you put a word that describes *you* and *your position*. Having done that, you are prepared to personalize the responsibility. The point is, the responsibility God has given you is yours to fulfill.

If you are unhappy with the people who work with you or the program you are in charge of, remember this: you are the one who must do something positive about the situation. The things we say about our people and programs are really statements about ourselves. It is time we took a good look at our own lives and determined to be the kind of leaders who make a positive difference.

What Type of Life Produces That Kind of Ministry?

Once again I remind you that what I say to myself, you must translate into a language that speaks to your own life. On this point, I can only share my own struggles and tell you I am in constant conflict with the world, the flesh, and the devil when it comes to becoming the kind of pastor I believe God wants me to be. The pressures of politics, time, and trouble make it anything but easy to live the sort of life that makes it possible for me to minister as I know I must.

I wish I could tell you I have found a formula for ordering my life into a just-right blend of togetherness with God and togetherness with people. Frankly, it is a constant struggle to find the balance I must have. But I am happy to tell you I'm learning more and more about the balance between being and doing. The people I preach to tell me they can see the difference when I discipline myself to be with the Lord in a way that makes me able to speak for Him with authority.

A long time ago, I heard about a preacher who was met every Sunday morning by an old man who asked him on his way to the pulpit, "Pastor, do you have a word from the Lord for us today?" The preacher said the old man's question was annoying at first but it became a blessing as it forced him to make sure he was really ready to preach. He realized that sermons were easy to write, but a message from the Lord came only through a process of spiritual searching and struggle.

One of our Sunday school teachers is a busy attorney. He is verbally gifted and mentally bright and it wouldn't take much time for him to get ready to speak for an hour. But he takes seriously his teaching ministry and I've seen his book-covered desk at home. I've been told he wouldn't think of entering his classroom without a minimum of 5 hours of preparation. Why? Because he knows he is arguing a case that will make an eternal difference.

Paul challenged the Romans not to be conformed to this world but to be transformed by the renewing of their minds. The same statement needs to be made to the church today. For it is only as we are transformed that we can become transformers.

There is no doubt about it, the world needs changing and the church of Jesus Christ is called to be the change agent in the world today. So let the church be the church! The world needs it now more than ever before.

7

People Grow Through Stages

We are born to grow. This is the first fact of life discovered by those who decide to follow the Lord. God's word to man in Jesus Christ was and is—"Let's get growing."

Robert Domeij

When I was a child, I spake as a child, I understood as a child, I thought as a child: but when I became a man, I put away childish things.

1 Corinthians 13:11

"Grow up!" he shouted. By the tone of voice Stephen used to say that to Stephanie, I knew something wasn't quite right. It had that sarcastic sound big brothers use when talking to little sisters whose antics disturb them. I could tell she had done something that displeased him, so he put her down by telling her to grow up.

His disapproval was explicit. But implicit in what he said was the idea that if she would only reach the ripe old age he had reached, her personality problems would disappear. Wouldn't it be wonderful if it really worked that way? Just reach a certain age and, presto, everything is A-okay.

But growth doesn't come automatically with age. Complex beings that we are, we must mature on the physical, intellectual, emotional, and spiritual levels if we are to be truly transformed and grow up to be the people God is calling us to be.

Luke indicates that Jesus grew up in every part of His personality. He said it this way: "And Jesus increased in wisdom and stature, and in favor with God and man" (Luke 2:52).

A man named Thomas Blandi concluded: "The purpose of life is spiritual, mental, and physical growth." I think we would all agree with that, and at the same time agree the evidence of growth in these areas isn't always easy to judge. Physical growth is a thing you can see and measure with a yardstick and with scales. Mental growth can be measured by certain testing tools, and we can grade the progress of our students on the basis of their answers to questions asked.

But how do you judge the spiritual? Well, you look for evidences of maturity or movement toward maturity. It is something a discerning teacher or leader can do, but in the final analysis the student must issue the pass/fail judgment and grade himself. If we are growing in Christ, there is a witness within; if not, there is a feeling of failure. The challenge is to constantly continue to reach for the goal of Christlike perfection, and call our students to follow us as we follow Jesus.

Ages and Stages

Standing before the congregation, I am sometimes devastated by the diversity. I know no two people to whom I will preach are on the same level. They aren't even who they were 1 week before. And there I stand with a simple message of hope that has grown out of my own struggle and offer it to them. I wonder at the Holy Spirit's ability to match the message to the men and women, boys and girls, who hear me preach it. And I am encouraged to realize God knows our growth rate and directs the ministry of the Holy Spirit toward our point of need.

Success is a moving target for those of us called to communicate the changeless Christ to a constantly changing world. Every church must come to grips with that reality and then respond to people where they are, as they are.

For us to do that, we must be patient and perceptive. We must patiently accept the difference between the ideal and the actual as our students grow in grace. A cute sign I saw in an office once pleaded: "Please be patient, God isn't finished with me yet." Certainly Jesus was patient with His first class of Christians. I think it was C. M. Ward who referred to them as the "dirty dozen." It isn't hard to understand this designation when you consider their carnal conduct. But Jesus loved them, and by being patient with them He brought them along toward spiritual maturity.

Another requisite is a perceptive eye. We need to see people as they are and understand what makes them tick. It is only as we become experts regarding our audience that we are able to communicate effectively with them.

Age-level Ministries

The normal church will minister to normal people who can be classified as children, youth, or adults. This fact should not be taken lightly. We will be effective in communicating Christ to these segments of our church family only as we make it part of our mission to know the people to whom we reach and preach. A gifted communicator knows not only what to say, but also how to say it. And he knows how to say it because he understands the people he is talking to. The ability to understand the audience is of utmost importance when it comes to communicating Christ.

Missionaries who go to foreign countries don't send ahead demanding the people there learn to speak

English for the comfort of the coming communicator. No, he goes to language school to learn how to speak in terms they understand. Only then does he attempt to speak, for only after giving attention to his audience and taking the time to learn the language of the learner, has he earned the right to be heard.

Ages

Those who work with the various age-groups in our churches should make it their passion to know all there is to know about their people. Preschool teachers should take every opportunity for training available so as to understand the children they minister to. And the same is true for every other age-group. We should be specialists in our departments.

In the following paragraphs, I will be making some observations about the church's ministries to the people who are growing through the various stages of this life. I hope what I say will serve as a starter and you won't stop learning about the special people who are a part of your teaching/learning assignment.

The Preschool People

According to Sandy Askew, a noted early childhood authority:

Exciting, pleasing, early experiences have a special significance for the young child for they are the beginnings, his initial relationships, his foundational experiences in his spiritual development. Good early experiences strengthen the child, they do not weaken him. In contrast, unsatisfactory early experiences weaken the child, rather than prepare him for a relationship with Jesus Christ (*Guiding the Preschool Child* [Springfield, MO: Gospel Publishing House, 1976], p. 1).

The importance of a quality ministry to the early

childhood or preschool segment of your church cannot be overstated. The 24- to 36-month stage is of utmost importance for it is during this time the child is building his "feelings file" from which he will draw his decisionmaking material in the future. Major decisions will be made rightly or wrongly on the basis of his learning experiences during these days. Don't assume the child is too young to learn. He is always aware and learning and we must make every effort to give the preschool child good experiences while at church.

Mel J. DeVries, author of *Guiding the Sunday School,* recently stated:

> The preschool years are foundational years in which the child is developing basic attitudes. This means the preschooler in Sunday school is forming attitudes about God, Jesus, the church, and himself. One of the goals of the preschool worker then is to help his students develop positive attitudes toward spiritual truths. . . .
>
> The total learning environment is especially important to the preschool child. He is very sensitive to his surroundings—the atmosphere of the room, the attitude of the workers, the actions and reactions of the other students. The preschooler is continually learning, and everything and everyone around him is teaching something *(Guiding the Sunday School* [Springfield, MO: Gospel Publishing House, 1977], pp. 45, 46).

A recent Mother's Day tribute was paid to a lady in our congregation known affectionately as Aunt Opal. For years, she has faithfully ministered to the 3-year-olds of our church. Even a casual observer can tell this lady loves those kids and they love her. I can't tell you how many times my own little girl has delayed our departure from church just to tell Aunt Opal good night once more.

When we surprised her with a special tribute, she

graciously accepted the tokens of love offered by the kids who clamored unceremoniously around her. Ellen Larson, our children's ministries director, made a few remarks. Then, with a quiet dignity, Opal asked if she could say a few words. Because she isn't known for her much talking, we were all a bit surprised and a hush fell on the audience.

Taking the hand-held microphone, she said, "This is the 32nd Mother's Day I wasn't supposed to have." She went on to tell how her doctor had one day broken the news to her that she had only a few weeks to live. She said she had smiled at the news and told the doctor of her request to God to grant her time to raise her children before she died. Her prayer had obviously been answered and some 32 Mother's Days later she was still making early childhood a warm and loving experience for our little ones.

I don't think there was a dry eye in the place as she walked down the aisle and back to her classroom with her little friends. In fact, she went out to a spontaneous standing ovation that still warms my heart just to hear it in my memory. I applaud every church and every person who shares the Sunday school Spirit of Jesus when He took the little children in His arms and blessed them.

I urge you to take a closer look at this important area of your church ministry, and ask: Are we doing our very best for the preschoolers?

The Elementary Child

Walk into an elementary classroom and you will quickly realize some things have changed since you sat where they now sit. Gone is the large picture roll that used to hide the crack in the wall of your basement classroom. In its place is a variety of media that makes you think being an elementary-age child in Sunday school today would be exciting. And you are right!

One of the most exciting changes is the redefined role of the teacher. No longer is the teacher the one who does all the talking. Now he or she guides the learning process; acting as a learning leader. This change is based on the realization that teachers may teach, but only learners can learn. The learning experience must involve the active participation of the learner, so involvement learning is the name of the game.

Ronald Clark, Elementary Specialist for the national Sunday School Department recently wrote:

> The role of the Sunday school teacher is changing. No longer is the traditional view of the teacher as a person who lectures to his class or shows the pupils how to do things valid. It is not unusual to walk into a Sunday school classroom and see children working together at interest centers or acting out a play they have written about the unit's lessons. It has been proven that children learn more by becoming involved in what they are hearing about. To meet the demand for increased knowledge, the role of the Sunday school teacher is becoming that of a guide who directs the children in discovering things for themselves (*Guiding the Elementary Child* [Springfield, MO: Gospel Publishing House, 1976], p. 34).

Those of us who minister to the children of our churches must learn to good-naturedly accept children as they are. Unreasonable demands from us will only aggravate the little problems they produce.

My wife's father was an insurance agent while she was growing up. As a well-dressed insurance man in those days, he had to wear a hat. She tells me either she or one of her brothers would sit on the hat almost every time they clamored into the car. She still remembers his oft-repeated remark in those moments of exasperation, "You can't have hats and kids."

If he had really had to make a choice between his hat and the kids, what do you think his decision would have been? Of course, he would have kept the children. Don't you think we churchmen ought to learn how to follow the example of our Lord and make the children comfortable in our churches? They do belong you know.

We need to remember the children in our churches and Sunday schools are experiencing rapid growth and are active. The "wiggles" are evidence of good health and should be welcomed. This means the children need room to learn and opportunity for physical movement.

Mentally, the child is gifted with a vivid imagination but has a very short interest span. For this reason, the child needs gentle, but firm guidance and multiple opportunities for encountering Biblical truth in a prepared environment.

Emotionally, the child in your church is sensitive to felt influences and needs loving relationships with Christians who really care. Socially, the child tends to be friendly but self-centered, so he needs both loving acceptance and opportunities to find out he really isn't the center of the universe.

Spiritually, our children are trusting and open to the love of God. We need to be sensitive to those times when the Holy Spirit is calling them to Christ and support them in their decisionmaking.

The people who effectively communicate with children observe the laws of *interest* (talk about things the child is interested in), *vocabulary* (use words the child can handle), and *explanation* (always take time to explain the unknown in terms of the known). Besides that, they honestly love the little people; and, more than anything else, it's that love that turns the child's heart toward the loving Lord Jesus Christ.

Youth

Burke said: "Tell me what are the prevailing sentiments that occupy the minds of your young men, and I will tell you what is to be the character of your next generation." Because we are concerned about the "church of tomorrow," we take seriously the church's ministry to its youth.

Those who minister to the young quickly realize this is a tough time in the life of a growing person. James Dobson described adolescence as a time of "indigestion, heartburn, and trauma." It is hard to tell whether it is the adolescent or his family and friends who suffer the most during this traumatic transition. Even the church feels a bit embarrassed by the uncomfortable teen in transition. The drums on the platform and "wild music" have tested the flexibility of more than one congregation. Torn between losing our youth and accepting the unacceptable, we wonder if valid youth ministry is possible. Of course the answer is "yes." If we really love them, it will show and even teenagers can't refuse the power of love.

Mel DeVries writes in *Guiding the Sunday School:*

The students will respect and respond to a teacher who has a real concern for them, who is open and honest with them, and who accepts them for what they are (p. 47).

The youth of your church are unique as a group and as individuals, but they have some common characteristics and needs we should be conscious of.

Physical growth continues through adolescence and the natural energy of this age demands opportunities for movement and activity. Mentally, our youth are capable of handling adult concepts—at least to a point. They should not be talked down to, but the wise teacher will understand they still lack the experience necessary to make the words they use have adequate meaning. Because they lack emotional maturity, teens are not always capable of adult responses to adult concepts.

Socially, the adolescent is beginning to move from a self-centered to an others-centered way of looking at his world. Spiritually, the opportunities are unlimited. Applying the laws of *patience* (loving acceptance), *presence* (availability without invasion), and *persistence* (faithful presentation of God's truth) we can make an eternal difference in the lives of young people today.

Ron McManus, Youth Ministries Specialist for the Assemblies of God, recently wrote:

> The adolescent is berated for many things, not the least of which is his tendency to abandon or question his religious heritage. He tends to lose interest in the church and seems to challenge the values and life-styles of Christians in the adult world. That world faces many problems, and often the adolescent is quite perplexed and confused as he moves through this period. The turmoils of adolescence are frustrating for adolescents and adults alike *(Guiding Youth* [Springfield, MO: Gospel Publishing House, 1976], p. 28).

Dr. David McKenna, President of Seattle Pacific College, says:

> Situational ethics is not an abstract theory on the campus; it is a reality. The absolutist stakes of the five fundamental sins—smoking, drinking, dancing, card playing, and movies—were pulled a long time ago. In their place are such questions as drugs, premarital sex, cheating, homosexuality, and suicide.

An observer of the youth scene once said it this way:

> Our youth today now love luxury. They have bad manners, contempt for authority, disrespect for older people. Children nowadays are tyrants. They no longer rise when their elders enter the room. They contradict their parents, chatter before company, gobble their food, tyrannize their teachers.

Before you add your loud "amen," let me tell you this was written in the fifth century B.C. and Socrates was the reporter!

The problems we face in ministry to youth aren't really all that new. Times and temptations have changed, but the basic nature of sinful man is the same and so is the solution. Salvation from our sinfulness is still offered through Jesus Christ, and the youth of today will respond to a real and loving Jesus if He is properly presented through the acts and attitudes of His church.

Adults

Somewhere along the line, Sunday school developed a "kids' stuff" image. Perhaps it started with Robert Raikes' "ragged schools" because his primary concern was the evangelism, education, and welfare of children. But whatever the cause, it is unfortunate that many adults today are missing a magnificent opportunity for spiritual growth because they think Sunday school has nothing to say or show to them.

During a recent review of my files, I found an article I had written in 1974 for the *Sunday School Counselor* about a class for young adults that was a going concern at that time. In it, I told about a young financial consultant who was a committed Christian, but a no-show for Sunday school until we began a series of studies on stewardship (that is church talk for money). To make a long story short, he was hooked by the subject and then stayed because the style of the class was "just what he was looking for."

The classes he had remembered (and wasn't about to return to) were straight lecture sessions and offered little or no opportunity for involvement. But this class was different. Instead of row after row of chairs lined up before a lectern, there were tables with chairs around them. And the lecture was a brief introduction of the Bible section being studied. The study was led by table leaders who were given guidelines and a specific assignment for the table group.

Besides the encounters with the Word of God, my friend found himself being introduced to many new friends as the table groups changed from week to week. He found himself inspired, instructed, and involved in these sessions, so he kept coming back for more.

Now both of us have moved to different towns and churches, but the last time I heard from him he was still excited about the study of God's great Book. Now he has young children and they are in Sunday school. And he doesn't just drop them off—he stays with them because he has discovered Sunday school is a delightful experience for adults too.

There are certain characteristics of adult learners that Christian educators must consider. Let me suggest four of them. First, adults enter the learning situation with other than learners' roles. The normal role of a child or young person is to be a learner, but adults are expected to be producers and doers. When these adults are talked down to or treated like children, they find their self-image threatened and try to escape or withdraw from such situations.

A second factor to consider is the experience adults bring to the classroom. This means they can speak from experience and have more to contribute through discussion.

Third on the list of considerations is the fact adult learners tend to be highly motivated and enter the classroom with a great deal of learning readiness. The pressures they live under make them want to know the answers to the questions they are asking. When a Sunday school class deals with the concerns the adult learners bring to the learning experience, they will be turned on by it. But if we talk about irrelevant and unimportant information, the attitude will be just the opposite.

A young preacher was accused by his congregation of answering questions nobody in the church was asking. That is not as funny as it is sad. Unfortunately, we have often failed to attract adult learners into our Sunday schools because we didn't listen carefully to the questions they were asking.

Finally, adults enter the learning experience with expectations of immediate application of learning. The truth they are handling isn't something they might use after they have "grown up." They are ready to do something with it right now, so every class should offer opportunity for an action response.

When ministering to adult learners, we should realize the principal points of the Tri-I Concept (inspiration, instruction, and involvement) are great guidelines for class sessions and lesson plans. After all, it was the method Jesus used with His men's class.

Mark 3:14 contains a record of the calling of the first class of disciples. The Bible says Jesus "ordained twelve, that they should be with him, and that he might send them forth to preach." You will note in this simple statement, two principles. The first is fellowship (that they should be with Him) and the second is purposeful training (that He might send them forth to preach).

I contend that the basic needs and wants of adults

are still the same today. We hunger for deep spiritual and real fellowship. We want to do something meaningful and significant with our lives. I believe the Sunday school of every church offers opportunities for meeting these needs and discipling adults today.

If we will observe the laws of *inspiration* (in-breathed divine life), *instruction* (systematic and purposeful instruction and training), and *involvement* (opportunities for experimenting with the born-again life-style), we will find the adults in our congregation more than interested in what we are offering in our Sunday school.

Paul wrote to the Ephesians about the gifts of the risen Christ and their purpose in His church. In the fourth chapter of his letter we read:

> And he gave some, apostles; and some, prophets; and some, evangelists; and some, pastors and teachers; for the perfecting of the saints, for the work of the ministry, for the edifying of the body of Christ: till we all come in the unity of the faith, and of the knowledge of the Son of God, unto a perfect man, unto the measure of the stature of the fullness of Christ: that we henceforth be no more children, tossed to and fro, and carried about with every wind of doctrine, by the sleight of men, and cunning craftiness, whereby they lie in wait to deceive; but speaking the truth in love, may grow up into him in all things, which is the head, even Christ: from whom the whole body fitly joined together and compacted by that which every joint supplieth, according to the effectual working in the measure of every part, maketh increase of the body unto the edifying of itself in love (Ephesians 4:11-16).

That really says it all, doesn't it? I especially like that part about "grow up into him." I think it is a grand goal for every pilgrim on the pathway of life. So let's get growing. It is the Sunday school spirit.

8

A Family Affair

The greatest danger to Christ's church is not infidelity or superstition. It is the spirit of worldliness in the homes of our Christian people, sacrificing the children to ambition or society, to the riches of the friendship of the world.

Andrew Murray

But whoso shall offend one of these little ones which believe in me, it were better for him that a millstone were hanged about his neck, and that he were drowned in the depth of the sea.

Matthew 18:6

1. "I'm too tired."
2. "We don't have enough money."
3. "Keep quiet!"

You have just read the winners (or should I say losers?) in a contest to determine the statements fathers use most in responding to their children. Delmar W. Holbrook, the compiler of the list, says they were the top three statements according to a survey of hundreds of children he talked to. Sort of scary, isn't it? Considering the family unit is the basic building block of Christian education, it seems we ought to be more careful about our communication in the home.

This chapter should begin with a strong statement regarding the obligation parents have to take an active part in discipling their children. Since the Sunday school only gets about 1 percent of their week—the rest going to the public school (16 percent) and the home (83 percent)—the responsibility for training our children belongs primarily to parents. Although there have been some exceptional miracles of mercy, generally the Sunday school cannot do what the home refuses to do. The Sunday school is just another tool for faithful parents to use in training the tender lives entrusted to them.

One of the most frustrating things about being a professional churchman is the tendency by some to hold exaggerated expectations regarding our ability to work miracles. This is also true for teachers in our Sunday schools. Parents who don't take time to teach and train their child during the week drop him off for 1 hour on Sunday morning for an injection of religious experience and moral training. It may be better than nothing, but is it good enough? I think not. We, as parents, must take seriously the training of our children. We cannot hold the church and Sunday school responsible until we have first accepted the primary responsibility.

When I was a Christian education director, I had a poster in my office that read: "We the willing are doing the impossible for the ungrateful. We have done so much for so long with so little, we are now qualified to do anything with nothing." An exaggeration? Of course it was, but I kept it around because I often got that frustrated feeling that poster seemed to communicate. I got it every time I thought of how few parents really expressed an obvious interest in the spiritual training of their own children.

Perhaps that is why I felt so good about something I read recently in *The Family Together* by Sharee and Jack Rogers:

The family is back in focus. After decades of being divided up, put down, and tossed aside, the family is again the center of attention. A recent Continental Congress on the family brought together more than 3,000 Christian workers to assess the status of the family. The press reported that two main conclusions emerged from a week of intense discussions. First, Christian leaders ought to spend more time with their own families, modeling what they hope to teach. Second, churches should reconsider their age-grouped ministries and seek ways to work with people in family units (Action House, Inc., Publishers, 1888 Century Park East, Suite 216, Los Angeles, California 90067).

The intergenerational Sunday school is only one of the radical ideas that have grown out of the increased interest in the family unit and its ministry. While I am skeptical about changing our age-level organizational approach, I do agree we must make every effort to support the family unit as it ministers to its individual members. This is consistent with my basic belief that the leadership of the church is called to minister to those who minister.

I don't think the ordinary church is mature enough for each family unit to fully accept the responsibility for Christian nurture. That is why I would be very uncomfortable with the idea of closing down our age-level ministries and Sunday schools. As we grow and reach out to the unsaved society around us, we will continue to be faced with the challenge of doing for some children and youth what their parents are either unable or unwilling to do. But, at the same time, we must stress the ministry of the family and offer training opportunities for the family units that express an interest in training for this task.

Ellen Larson, Christian education director for First Assembly of God in Santa Ana, California, recently wrote:

Each family member strongly influences every other family member. Therefore, to minister to the whole person, Christian educators must minister to families. Any Sunday school which teaches a pupil without regard for the rest of his family cannot be totally effective. The opportunity to minister to the family as a unit is a challenge which must be accepted.

The church in Long Beach, California, pastored by my friend T. Ray Rachels, recently experimented with a one-Sunday "intergenerational Sunday school." Candy Jones, children's ministries director, and the Christian education committee of the church worked together to plan and promote the project which the pastor called "very successful and profitable." He went on to say, "We all learned a lot about ourselves and our need to learn to live the good news in our family."

While such efforts are most encouraging and we are hearing a lot about family-life ministries, I am afraid we've got a long way to go before we can truly tell people our Christian education program is "home-made."

I am forced to face this fact when I hear from a major publisher of family-life ministry materials that the response has been disappointing and Christian education directors complain that projected family-life enrichment efforts have received only slight support from church leaders. Let's face it—any ministry is easier said than done and to experience success in this area we will have to expend a tremendous amount of energy and effort. But before we do, we should decide whether or not the result is worth the effort.

I think the answer is obvious. The family was God's idea in the beginning and even a glance at the Bible will reveal God's great concern for the family unit. Obviously, there is a tremendous need for family-oriented ministries today and the results experienced by those who have responded to the need is argument enough for making a family plan a part of your Sunday school strategy.

Something Can Be Done!

The old saying, "Where there's a will, there's a way," suggests that first a decision to do something in support of our family units must be made. No program will be successful unless leadership is determined to make it successful. Once the decision is made, then ways to make family-life ministry happen will begin to appear. Gifts the church can give the family units will begin to be discovered, to everyone's delight.

The Gift of Time

Pointing to the bulletin the pastor said, "Look at that! We've got something going every night this week." From the way he said it you could tell he was proud of his church that was busy for the Lord. And when he was challenged about the correctness of such a crowded calendar, it became obvious he had given little thought to the needs of his own family or the other families in his church.

Just a little while ago, my work on this book was interrupted by my three favorite people. My wife and two children came in to say good night and check out the stormy weather outside. My window looked out on the rain-drenched *cul-de-sac* glistening in the light of a street lamp and, with little regard for my privacy, they piled in and took positions at the window like the Rose Parade was about to pass by. Since they had unhooked my train of thought, I decided to turn out the desk lamp and watch it rain with them. In the darkness of that room, I saw the truth I'm telling you now better than when the light was on.

I saw in the shadowy room three people who are my primary parishioners. I can't resign from that congregation. I must love them, teach them, and bring them up to know God. Then I thought of hundreds of other family units in our congregation and realized I must never make them so busy with pointless programs that they don't have time just to be together as a family.

A wise man once urged, "Beware of the barrenness of a busy life." I would add, "Guard against the cramming of calendars so your family doesn't have time to be together." Give them the gift of time by setting aside one night when nothing happens at the church and urge families to spend that time caring and sharing experiences.

The Gift of Training

It isn't good enough just to clear the calendar and give your families the gift of a free night. Unless they know what to do with that time, it will be wasted. To keep that from happening, we must provide support in the dual forms of tools and training.

The tools are relatively easy to come by. Our religious publishing houses are making much quality material available and we can't complain about the lack of curriculum support. The only thing we have to worry about is the process of moving this material into the home.

Some churches do this by subscribing to family-life publications for their people. Others reprint materials and promote family home nights through their bulletins and special mailings.

A very successful idea we once used involved a family-style dinner during a well-planned and promoted family-life festival. We set up displays and booths where information and consultants were available around the circumference of the room in which the meal was served.

But tools are only tools until the workmen are trained in their use of them. That is why many churches are experimenting with things like the intergenerational Sunday school hour I mentioned earlier. Also being used successfully are training classes and retreats. To be successful, these sessions must include opportunities for experimenting with the materials and ideas as well as being introduced to them.

Howard Hendricks, author of *Heaven Help the Home* (Wheaton, IL: Victor Books, 1974), recently said:

> We are surrounded by foreign, hostile, and home-shattering influences in our world today. The supportive elements of society no longer feed or shade us. The Christian home must bloom in a field of weeds.

Whether we realize it or not, our homes are hurting and the local church must minister at this point of great need. When we do, it will begin to make a noticeable change in our churches.

Richard Baxter was one preacher who transformed his church through his personal ministry to individual family units. He was the pastor of a wealthy and sophisticated church in England and his first 3 years of ministry were without visible results. Then he said:

> I threw myself across the floor in my study and cried out to God, "God, you must do something with these people, or I'll die." . . . It was as if God spoke to me audibly and said, "Baxter, you're working in the wrong place. You're expecting revival to come through the church. Try the home."

That is when Richard Baxter began a home-to-home ministry helping his people set up family altars and getting their priorities right. Of course, revival came; not over night, but soon.

I feel completely comfortable in promising that if you and your church will put the priority on ministry to the family unit, it won't be long before a revival breaks out in your congregation.

The local church and the family unit are a dynamic duo. When one ministers to the other, the echo principle is experienced and both are enriched. So support your family units. It is the Sunday school spirit!

9
Beyond the Classroom

When the building complex and the church con-
stituency become the field in which to work rather than
a force with which to work, the church is in trouble.

Hollis L. Green

To the weak became I as weak, that I might gain the
weak: I am made all things to all men, that I might by
all means save some.

1 Corinthians 9:22

There is a world of difference between church work
and the work of the church. Church work is what we
do to get ourselves ready to go out and do the work of
the church. Sermons, songs, and Sunday school are just
part of the preparation (church work) for fulfilling our
purpose (the work of the church).

Emil Brunner said: "The church exists by mission
as fire exists by burning." Without a clear understanding of our purpose our meetings lose their meaning
and church becomes a duty rather than a delight.

A comedian who had obviously missed the point of
Sunday school recently made the caustic comment,
"Church was that weekly reminder that there was at
least one thing worse than going to school." I'm afraid
many church attenders are enduring the church experience because they haven't taken hold of the truth
concerning the purpose of our gathering together.

Samuel Eliot argued: "A church should be a power

house where sluggish spirits can get recharged and re-animated." But recharged and reanimated for what? We must answer this before we can get to the point. The first law of power is purpose and the secret to discovering the divine dynamic is understanding the divine design.

In his book *Why Churches Die* (Minneapolis: Bethany Fellowship, Inc., 1972), Hollis Green writes: "The basic premise undergirding the advance of Christianity is that the church must accept the responsibility for carrying the message of Christ to people outside the four walls of the church building." Ah, there it is! Evangelism is our purpose and we prepare for it through our fellowship with fellow believers in the context of the local church.

When we come together with the understanding that we are preparing to fulfill our purpose, the meeting has a point. It is when we realize church work is just a means to an exciting end called evangelism that the getting-ready experience is charged with a holy excitement. There must be an excitement about the challenge beyond the four walls of the church before what happens inside the four walls is charged with the power of purpose.

Mark's remarks about the calling of the disciples by Jesus reveals He called them together to send them forth. They were to be *with* Him, but they were also to be sent *from* Him. He never lost sight of His reason for being. He was working all the time to reach out to the faraway folk through the few up-close friends He had called.

Hollis Green observed:

> When the building complex and the church constituency become the field in which to work rather than a force with which to work, the church is in trouble. . . . Church ministries should be designed to expand the church beyond

the building complex to take the message of saving grace to the community *(Why Churches Die*, Hollis L. Green [Minneapolis: Bethany Fellowship, Inc., 1972], pp. 42, 43).

Ephesians 4:11, 12 is a much misunderstood part of the Bible. Too many people read it as a statement of fact that ministers have been called to serve the church and they are to do three things: "the perfecting of the saints," "the work of the ministry," and "the edifying of the body of Christ." Frankly, when I read it their way I feel an overpowering urge to write my letter of resignation and quit. After all, I haven't been able to perfect the pastor. So how can I hope to perfect the parishioners?

But when I read it the right way, my "nerve" is renewed. I find the harsh word *perfecting* modified by the more believable "maturing" and, instead of a three-fold task, I realize I am called to accomplish one thing which then produces two results. But before I say more about this passage, look at it as it appears in the *New International Version:*

It was he [Christ] who gave some to be apostles, some to be prophets, some to be evangelists, and some to be pastors and teachers, to prepare God's people for works of service, so that the body of Christ may be built up.

That statement is really simple and the strategy it proposes is powerful. First, the minister called to do church work is to minister in a way that matures the members of the church for a ministry of communicating Christ. As the members exercise their ministry gifts, the church is edified and strengthened.

For far too long, the professional clergy has communicated by its conduct that the membership was to come to church, observe the efforts of the preacher, pay the bills, and bring a friend from time to time so the Lord and the preacher could get a shot at his soul. Lately, there seems to be a recovery of the truth stated by Paul concerning the ministry of all the members. The liberation of the laity is a delight to behold and where the Ephesian formula is being followed, there are dynamic bodies of believers springing up.

A New York church ran a statement on its outdoor bulletin board which listed the "ministers" as "all the members" of the congregation. Underneath there was a line that read, "Assistants to the ministers—The Pastoral Staff."

The secret of success is not the superstar approach, but the servant strategy that ministers to those who minister. I am confident that each church contains the seeds of a powerful presentation of the gospel of Christ to a watching world. All that is needed is for the leadership of the church to inspire, instruct, and involve its ministering members.

Inspiring, Instructing, Involving

I think there are three steps that will take us far beyond the walls of our sanctuaries. They are the three steps of the Tri-I Concept and a self-repeating strategy for evangelism or discipling.

First, we must make people aware that they are somebody and they can do something. A heavy emphasis on the giftedness of the congregation will be necessary to counteract the "laity" idea. There is an unfortunate mind-set in many congregations that causes the people in the pew to look up to the preacher and down on themselves. Somehow the pastor must make his people aware that they are gifted and called of God.

I watched this truth impact on the members of two congregations in recent years and it was amazing the change it produced in the people. It made a dynamic difference in the way they worshiped and their work became powerfully productive. I simply told them (over and over and over again) God had given them special abilities and gifts and they should seek God for His direction in the use of their gifts. Ministries I never dreamed of developed as the result of pushing the people into a face-to-face confrontation with the call from God. I had more people than I care to count resign from positions I had asked them to take, but I can't recall a single resignation from a person who had prayed through to a call from God to a ministry in the church.

All we try to do is challenge the congregation to consider the possibility of meaningful ministry. When the call comes, we call it *inspiration* and move on to stage two—*instruction*.

Once the ministering member of the church expresses his sense of call, we must give the necessary training and counsel. Each call is unique, but there is a general pattern of training that applies to all ministries. The pastor, or those he trains, must take a personal responsibility for the development of each ministry. A solid and steady program of spiritual development through regular worship, Bible study, and fellowship is the first part of the package. Then, the new ministering member must be discipled to be cooperative and submissive to the leadership God has placed over him. This is often a difficult lesson to learn, but any ministry that does not submit to authority loses its effectiveness by the very act of rebellion.

Finally, the ministry gifts that surface should be *involved* in the ministry of the local church. Some of the best programs in the church today are those that resulted from someone seeing a need and seeking to fill it. Of course, they had to be allowed to do something in the church by leadership that was not overly jealous or too control-oriented.

I am afraid many of us pastors are guilty of frustrating our parishioners because it is easier to hire a staff of paid workers than to motivate a team of volunteers. The problem with that is the limiting effect. Our church will only be as big and dynamic as the staff can make it. On the other hand, there is no limit to what can happen if we let our people go where the people are.

We must be encouraging and supportive with those of our number who are called to a special field of endeavor. All it will cost us is a little consideration and creativity and the results will be beyond belief.

Because an ounce of application is worth a ton of *abstraction,* let me tell you about several successful ministries that go beyond the Sunday school hour and the four walls of the sanctuary. They are ministries that fulfill the purpose of evangelism and tend to turn on those involved.

Bus Ministry

Some of the superchurches of today have become what they are by using buses to bring in the people. So much has already been written and said about this phenomenal ministry, I won't take time to go over ground that has already been covered by people like my friend Daniel Johnson who wrote the book *Building With Buses* (Grand Rapids: Baker Book House). I will just stop long enough on the subject to say that, in my opinion, the greatest thing about bus ministry is it offers people a plan for confronting their neighbors and neighborhoods with a simple and systematic gospel witness.

Once the basic presentation has been mastered, the door-to-door canvasser begins to feel more comfortable with the idea of walking up to a door and introducing himself, his church, and his Lord. It is a plan that works when people work it and the conversions and dramatic growth in places where the plan is implemented testify to its effectiveness. While I won't go so far as to say it is the only way to win the world—as a few bus enthusiasts seem to suggest—I will agree it is a powerful tool. It's church work that lets the people do the work of the church.

Neighborhood Bible Study

Another strategy that works well is sort of busing in reverse. Instead of trying to get the people in through a highly promotional approach, the church sends out the saints to "salt" the community with small-group meetings. Each group has its own personality and every sponsoring church has its own system for controlling this ministry.

There are basically two types of neighborhood strategies. One is child-oriented while the other is adult in style. Under the heading "child-oriented neighborhood meetings," I would put all "children" who live at home. Under the "adult" heading, I would put all programs that aim at those who are out in the world on their own and those responsible for households.

Child-oriented Neighborhood Strategies

Among the neighborhood programs that work well with children are weekly Bible club meetings, released-time education, and neighborhood VBS programs. Through these efforts, we are able to reach neighborhood children who would never enter a church on their own. These programs offer an opportunity for concerned Christians to let their "light shine" in the place God has put them. They understand the people they are ministering to better than an expert from another place could ever hope to. I like this idea because it seems to move us away from our institutional Christianity and makes it more of a grass roots sort of thing.

Adult-oriented Neighborhood Strategies

First, we should define neighborhood. For adults, it is obviously bigger than the area where their home is. The place they work is a neighborhood and the people they work with are their neighbors, just like those they live next to. So Bible studies and evangelistic efforts can occur in any of these places.

Lunch-hour Bible-study groups on the job are becoming more and more common. Neighborhood fellowship groups are experiencing some exciting happenings as people get together around God's Word.

My wife Pat started a weekly Wednesday morning Word study in 1976. It has attracted an enrollment of 125 ladies and an average of 60 ladies meet each week on our campus at this writing. The secret to her success has been a steady emphasis on systematic Bible study and the transdenominational nature of the program. About 40 percent of the ladies attend other churches. According to Pat: "The thing that excites me most about Word Study is the way we have grown beyond our own church. The girls have brought neighbors and now the neighbors are bringing friends and neighbors—there is no limit to what can be accomplished as we continue to reach out."

The morning begins with a 15-minute session that includes singing, a planned testimony, and prayer. Then the women divide into groups of 10 to 15 to discuss the questions they have studied at home. The last 30 minutes of the 1½-hour program is an inspirational lecture from the portion of Scripture that has been studied. Occasional "evangelistic luncheons" with featured outside speakers add a special touch to the program and expose other ladies to the weekly study.

One of the prime reasons for the success of the ministry is its involvement of the ladies involved. Each group leader works under the guidance of the leader and is responsible for calling every lady in the group each week. She also forms a prayer chain among the ladies in her group. Once again, the idea of moving people toward people is obvious. It is the strategy of evangelism; going with the gospel; taking it to the streets.

The old-fashioned street meetings aren't as obvious as they once were. A good tambourine player is hard to find in most of our churches today. But that doesn't mean we have lost our evangelistic zeal. The methods may have changed, but the message and motivation are still the same.

St. Jerome called baptism the ordination of the laity. Every member is a minister and has a ministry. It will require a creative and caring congregation to liberate each layman to ministry, but it is the only way to get the job done. One man in one pulpit isn't enough. Every member must break out of the box we call our building and take the news to his neighborhood. He must preach and proclaim it in a language the neighborhood natives understand.

Paul evidenced the creative mind-set of the adaptive Christian communicator when he confessed: "To the weak became I as weak, that I might gain the weak: I am made all things to all men, that I might by all means save some" (1 Corinthians 9:22).

If we are to exercise the creative Christian communication ministries required to fulfill the Great Commission in this day and time, we must replace the seven last words of the church: "We've never tried it that way before," with the seven first words of spiritual success: "I can do all things through CHRIST."

10

The More Things Change

The future has a habit of suddenly and dramatically becoming the present.

Roger Babson

Teaching them to observe all things whatsoever I have commanded you: and, lo, I am with you alway, even unto the end of the world. Amen.

Matthew 28:20

That last line of Matthew's Gospel is as comforting as the lines before it are challenging. Having placed an unbearable burden of responsibility on the disciples, Jesus ends by assuring them of His supportive presence, "even unto the end of the world."

Last-day disciplers should delight in the realization that we aren't alone. Jesus Christ, the Great Discipler, is still standing with us. In fact, He is *within* us and working through us by the powerful presence of the Holy Spirit. Considering the magnitude of the mission, we do well to remember the only pressure we are under is the responsibility to be obedient. He does not ask for our ability, just our availability. When we give Him that He gives us His power. We make ourselves available and He makes us able.

Isaiah, the evangelical prophet, began his powerful proclamation ministry with a simple statement of availability, "Here am I. Send me!" That's when the Lord said, "Go, and tell."

Times have changed tremendously since the sending of Isaiah and the days of the disciples but there are at least two constants. First, the Lord still looks for obedient people to go with the gospel. Second, those who accept the challenge are comforted by His presence and energized by His power. Even in this anxious age these ageless anchors still secure us.

The More Things Change

I've listened to the doomsday declarations about dying dollars, conspiring computers, and energy shortages and been depressed. Then I've tuned in a media missionary and been told I should send more money fast because this is the greatest day of opportunity the world has ever had. It all leaves me a bit confused and thinking the best thing about the future is it can only come one day at a time.

Patrick Henry once said, "I know no way of judging the future but by the past." Using that formula the only thing I can tell you for certain about tomorrow is it will come and God will be in it. It probably won't be as bad as the prophets of doom predict or as good as the optimists promise. But it will be a day we must take advantage of and do the work of God in.

Louise Haskins penned something that blesses me whenever I'm troubled about tomorrow. Facing a new year she wrote:

> I said to the man who stood at the gate of the year: Give me a light that I may tread safely into the unknown. And he replied: Go out into the darkness, and put thine hand into the hand of God. That shall be to thee better than light and safer than a known way.

The argument I make for not worrying about tomorrow doesn't mean we shouldn't see it coming and get ready for it. The Chinese have a saying: "He who could foresee affairs three days in advance would be rich for thousands of years." That may be an exaggeration but the man who can anticipate the opportunities that will come tomorrow is more likely to enjoy success than the man who doesn't.

When Charles Kettering was questioned about his planning he explained: "I expect to spend the rest of my life in the future, so I want to be reasonably sure of the kind of future it's going to be."

It goes without saying the time to plan for the future is the present. We must get ready for tomorrow today or when it arrives we will spend it chasing yesterday. Roger Babson was right when he observed: "The future has a habit of suddenly and dramatically becoming the present."

Is There a Sunday School in Our Future?

In 1978 I was privileged to sit as a member of the national Sunday School Committee of the Assemblies of God when we brainstormed about Christian education in the 1980's. The other day I was reading the minutes of that meeting and smiled when I saw the words of my fellow pastor and friend, Kenneth Mayton from Atlanta, Georgia. He had said: "With the nearing of the Sunday school's 200th birthday, hopefully growth, quantitatively and qualitatively, will be seen." Then he said, "The future is bright, I think." What brought the smile was the addition of those two little words, "I think."

I think it's a good idea for anyone who writes or talks about the future to underscore the less-than-certain nature of his predictions by adding an occasional, "I think." What follows are some of the thoughts and opinions expressed by the members of that group of guessers. Although we like to think we are better able than most to speak on the subject due to our experience and the available data, we realize the future is foggy, even though we're only looking the distance of a decade. So with that cautious disclaimer I will tell you some of the things we see in the distance.

Discovery learning will continue to be promoted by knowledgeable Christian educators. Those who have learned about learning will realize the learner must learn and the teacher's role is that of a learning leader. Curriculum support and teacher-training programs will reflect this belief and the learning experience will become more of a delight than a drag for the learner.

Family-life ministries will be stressed. After a slow start the Christian education leaders in our churches will begin to get the idea across and young families will start to cooperate with the institutional Sunday school instead of depending on it as the sole source of Biblical instruction.

Special groups within the church family will be given special attention because of the unique nature of their needs. Programs for exceptional children and single adults will become more acceptable in local churches and efforts will be made to pull these people into the mainstream of church life.

Age-level specialists such as children's ministries directors will increase in number. The change from program-centered structuring (horizontal organization) to people-centered structuring (vertical or age-level organization) will increase the demand for age-level experts.

Teacher training and staff enrichment efforts will be increased. Churches will face the fact that promotions may bring in big crowds but a real congregation must be built one member at a time and that will demand a discipling emphasis and leadership training.

Church growth will be defined more honestly and realistically. The idea of judging the greatness of a church on the basis of Sunday school attendance or missions giving or any other single factor will give way to a total-church view when it comes to evaluating.

The for-kids-only image of the Sunday school will continue to give way to a growing awareness that the weekly Bible study session has much to offer adults too. Adult Christian education opportunities will be more ministry-oriented and aim to produce evangelistic activity and mobilize the members of the church for ministry.

Busing and transportation evangelism may be bothered by fuel shortages, and church schedules may have to be changed due to restricted travel. But there is a confidence that creative churchmen will find a workable formula, for where there's a will there's always a way.

During the sessions that produced these "I think" statements we faced some hard facts and considered some ominous trends. But the attitude was generally positive. I think all the members of that group must have been true believers and Sunday school enthusiasts. I say that because the bottom-line conclusion was that Sunday schools will not only survive, but also thrive as we move closer to the coming of Christ. The methods will be changed to meet the needs of modern man but the message will remain unchanged and the Sunday school spirit will stay strong.

It was interesting to us that the magazine that had called the weekly Sunday school session the most wasted hour of the week and had predicted its demise has itself died. Apparently, the Sunday school movement is more full of life than *Life* magazine. It seems to have a great tolerance for abuse and refuses to fold.

But that doesn't mean we should take our Sunday

schools for granted. George Edgerly, Research and Field Services Coordinator for the national Sunday School Department, returned from a meeting of church statisticians in 1978 with a sobering report. He noted the continuing decline of mainline Protestant denominations and pointed to an almost positive correlation between liberality in doctrine and the decrease in size and strength. He also called attention to the fact that a de-emphasis of Christian education is followed by an identical curve in membership approximately 5 years later.

His conclusion was that the major denominations are now reaping the seeds they sowed 15 to 20 years ago in decrying the value of Sunday school. He observed:

> I came away from the meeting with a renewed conviction of the role of Christian education generally, and the Sunday school in particular, in the continued growth of the church. It is apparent that many denominations who moved away from emphasizing Sunday school two decades ago are awaking to discover a generation has been lost to their church. I am personally alarmed by the beginning trend of some in our own movement to discount the effectiveness of the role of Christian education in building the congregation. One thing is certain, preaching and worship must be balanced by teaching and nurture. If we do not, we will not conserve the results of the present enthusiasm of worship and revival of evangelism.

Not Prophecies, Just Predictions

I don't write as a prophet in the foretelling sense of the word, but I do have a few predictions to put forward at this point. These educated guesses grow out of my understanding of God's Word and what I see happening around me.

Times will get tougher. In spite of the hopeful promises of the politicians, it seems we are sinking deeper into the quicksand of human failure. The more we struggle to solve our problems the worse our situation becomes. Because mankind has refused the Source of salvation, we are sliding faster and faster toward our final failure.

The Bible predicts things will "wax worse and worse" as we approach the windup. We might as well brace ourselves and get ready. The worst is yet to come. And that's good news. That means our redemption is drawing near and there has never been a better time to preach the gospel.

The bad news is the world is on a collision course with catastrophe. But the good news is that in times like these the opportunities for evangelism are enlarged. Missionary-evangelist Otis Keener recently told our congregation, "Because the world is at its worst the church must be at its best."

The darker the night the brighter the light shines. Because of the increase of wickedness there is a growing demand for the good news the church of Jesus Christ is preaching. Things will continue to get worse in the world but that will make things better for the true church of Jesus Christ.

Our ministries and message will be simplified. In a world that is becoming incredibly complex, the church is being called to communicate a Christ who offers a simple solution. Many who have stumbled over the simplicity of the gospel before are beginning to face the fact that salvation is offered not to those who understand but to those who believe.

The church has too often confused people by majoring on minors and minoring on majors. May God help us to recover the simple truth if we've lost it. If we've only neglected it, I pray we will return to a faithful and fervent presentation of Jesus Christ, Son of God and Saviour.

I'm told Karl Barth was asked during a postlecture question-and-answer session, "What is the most profound concept you've ever considered in your quest for truth?" With but a moment's hesitation he replied, "Jesus loves me, this I know, for the Bible tells me so."

I preach week after week to people who are a lot smarter than I am when it comes to the things that make this world of ours so complex. But they come to hear the preaching of the simple salvation story and the good news about Jesus Christ. Why? Because it's the missing part of the puzzle. Without it their life isn't complete.

Some time ago I visited the widowed wife of a missionary. She was hospitalized and I had gone to cheer her with a pastoral visit. In the course of our conversation I said, "You've probably heard everything I could tell you about the faithfulness of God hundreds of times before." That's when she squeezed my hand and with a weak smile said, "Tell me again. It does me good to hear it."

Some of us seem to think we have to keep coming up with something new or at least a new way of saying the same old thing. Not so! Whether we teach or preach we should strive for simplicity and faithfulness to the basic truth taught by the gospel. Remember, Jesus Christ comes through best when the presentation is uncluttered.

Our methods will change. As certainly as I predict our simple message won't change, I predict our methods will change. Although we hate change, it is the price of progress. Until the end of time man will continue to develop new and better tools that will alter our methodology. Just take a look at the last 50 years and you'll see how differently we do things today.

Another factor that forces change is the life-style of the people we are called to communicate Christ to. Techniques that worked well in other places and times just don't fit in the here and now. So we have to keep moving with the people we minister to. Sure it's uncomfortable and I often wish for the simple, quiet time of those good old days but success is a moving target. We cannot stand still, stamp our feet, and demand the calendar be turned back to a time that suits our style. Our style must be changed to fit the time. The man who marries today will be a widower tomorrow. The message is clear: adapt or perish!

Niccolo Machiavelli observed: "There is nothing more difficult to take in hand, more perilous to conduct, or more uncertain of its success, than to take the lead in the introduction of a new order of things." Anyone who has served in a place of leadership and acted as a change agent would say "amen!" to that statement.

It's never pleasant to be the person on the point. Those who follow us would much rather stay with the status quo and standard procedures, and our constant call to something more is often annoying to them.

Frequently I have ended Christian education conferences with a presentation titled "How to Change Your Program and Live to Tell About It." It may sound like a silly session but I'm dead serious about the importance of leading people forward at a pace that is patient and productive. I've seen too many overanxious, eager change agents make a mess of things because they didn't understand human nature.

Writing in *Dun's Review of Modern Industry*, Ralph M. Besse, Executive Vice-president of Cleveland Electric Illuminating Company, gave these 10 fundamental facts concerning change.

1. Change is more acceptable when it is understood than when it is not.
2. Change is more acceptable when it does not threaten security than when it does.

3. Change is more acceptable when those affected have helped to create it than when it has been externally imposed.

4. Change is more acceptable when it results from an application of previously established impersonal principles than it is when it is dictated by personal order.

5. Change is more acceptable when it follows a series of successful changes than it is when it follows a series of failures.

6. Change is more acceptable when it is inaugurated after prior change has been assimilated than when it is inaugurated during the confusion of other major change.

7. Change is more acceptable if it has been planned than if it is experimental.

8. Change is more acceptable to people new on a job than to people old on the job.

9. Change is more acceptable to people who share in the benefits of change than to those who do not.

10. Change is more acceptable if the organization is trained to plan for improvement than it is if the organization is accustomed to static procedures.

One of the worst mistakes made by would-be change agents is changing programs without first changing people. Old schedules are scrapped in favor of an experimental one, new equipment is installed, and even the terminology is changed, but the people stay the same. Little wonder things keep going wrong and the routine returns to the old rut.

When it comes to change, the bottom-line truth is we must change people and then changed people will change things. It's a matter of educating. First the people must *know* there is a better way. Then they must *feel* strongly they should adopt the better way. When they feel this way they will *do* what needs to be done to move out of the past and into the present.

Changing times require a special sort of leadership that is sure of its footing and flexible enough to stretch to touch a world that tends to be moving beyond the reach of the rigid churchman.

Men will make the difference. If there is a Sunday school in our future it will be there because dedicated men and women decide to put it there. Just as Robert Raikes planted one in Gloucester in 1780, we must decide this time and place needs a witness and pay the price it requires.

We may have first-class facilities and excellent curriculum support, but if we don't have people who care enough to reach and teach through our Sunday schools, we are wasting our money and efforts. That's why I believe so strongly in leadership development and urge churches to make an all-out effort to produce personnel.

We need an unlimited supply of teachers who know God and know people and know how to bring them together in an encounter that produces eternal life change. These indispensable people must be men and women of knowledge, skill, and Christian concern. It's my belief that a teacher who cares will do what needs to be done to acquire the necessary knowledge and skills. The main problem we face today is not a knowledge but a motivational problem.

Howard Hendricks tells the story of an elderly lady he met while teaching in a Sunday school convention in Chicago. She was over 80 years old and the teacher of a class of 13 boys in a small church with 55 members. Considering her remarkable success, Hendricks wondered why she would bother to ride a bus all night at her own expense to attend a convention. When he asked her why she was attending the convention, she told him she hoped to learn something that would make her a better teacher.

He was moved by her dedication and later told the story of his encounter with her. One of his listeners introduced Hendricks to the remarkable record of this little lady who cared. It seems more than 80 young men who passed under her influence found their way into the Christian ministry. That's the sort of thing that happens when someone is truly consecrated to the cause of communicating Christ. The passion of our heart is of far greater importance than the natural gifts or acquired knowledge we possess.

The Best of Times, the Worst of Times

"It was the best of times. It was the worst of times." That's how Charles Dickens begins his famous historical novel *A Tale of Two Cities*. Any historian could use that lead line to begin the story of any time and any place. Even in the worst oppression there is opportunity and in the best of times there is the tragic evidence of man's inhumanity to man.

I'm told the nostalgia craze of today is an evidence of our desire to escape into our past. Because the present is too tough and the future is terrifying, we try to cope by reaching back into our yesterdays to relive an experience we were able to live through.

Janette Strutchen, a favorite poet of mine, spoke to this point when she wrote about the people whose shock absorbers were shot and wanted to back up to the "good old days." Then she asked what was so good about the good old days. Her question provoked me to reminisce and to realize while things have changed tremendously they have tended to stay the same. The pains and problems of the past seem slight and simple from where I stand right now, but at the time they were just like the ones I'm struggling with today. The scene has changed and this actor has aged but the story line is stable.

The Scene Has Changed

My earliest memories are of growing up in a parsonage in Pratt, Kansas. We had 8,000 people in town and a church family of over 200. It was easy to get to know people in that time and place. I remember the simple pleasures of Saturday suppers of hamburgers, French fries, and my own chilled bottle of Pepsi Cola. There followed the inevitable Saturday night bath and Sunday school lesson study. Then came the reward of getting to listen to the first half-hour of the Grand Ole Opry on the big radio in the front room.

Sunday was a day for Sunday school, church, and an outing on one of the members' farms if I could talk Mom into letting me go home with them. The Sunday night experience featured a rousing service of spirited singing and powerful preaching. I must confess that while my preacher father sweated through his sermon, I often slept. Not that he wasn't a good preacher—in fact, I think he's the best I've ever heard. The problem was, I was played out from a day in the great outdoors.

I can still remember the satisfied feeling of coming home after a Sunday afternoon in the country. We'd top the hill to see the lights and landmarks I'd gotten to know so well. And it wasn't hard to find the church on Hamilton Street, we just went right to it. It was all so beautifully simple then.

That's not the way it is today. I really realized that on a recent Saturday night when I was flying home. The day had started in New York and was about to end in Los Angeles. As the plane began its glide into the L.A. basin, I looked out the window and saw the mind-boggling sight of a sea of lights that seemed to stretch forever. We dropped a little lower and I could make out the flowing freeways and was rudely reminded of the long drive home through all that traffic that was still ahead of me. That's when I thought to myself, "What's a nice guy like you doing in a place and time like this?"

Of course, the answer I gave myself had to do with God's call and obedience to His direction for my ministry. But even as I talked to myself I realized how I had been changed by the changing times. Not only had the scenery shifted from a rural, small-town setting to a major city backdrop, but the actor had also aged. I wasn't the kid I used to be and I might as well face the fact I couldn't go home again. I couldn't call back the easier, simpler times when the pressures were all my dad's and the pleasures were all mine.

Then I saw the story line is still unchanged. Like my father before me, I'm in the ministry and living out the divine drama of God's search for sinners. The message hasn't changed a bit. God is still saying, "I love you," to a lost world through those who will hear and heed His call.

Norman Vincent Peale, the famous preacher and writer, recently wrote the following remembrance:

> My preacher father was a terrific man. He never used notes when preaching a sermon. He studied long hours. He worked hard, then he preached out of his big mind and heart. And he loved people. One time I found him sitting on a curbstone in Columbus, sobbing. "Dad, what in the world is wrong with you?" I asked. "I've been out visiting the people and their sorrows and troubles break my heart." I sat down on the curb beside him, put my arm around him. Always later I hoped that God would give me that much love for people.
>
> Perhaps it was the experience of seeing him standing in the pulpit Sunday after Sunday, loving the people and preaching the gospel of the unsearchable riches of Christ, that made me decide to follow his example rather than do anything else in the world.
>
> When preparing my first sermon I asked my father what in the world I would say. His reply was practical and down

to earth. "In the first place," he said, "don't try to show off. Don't try to make the people think you know something, because you know you don't." Then he said something that has affected my entire ministry. "Just tell the people that God loves them." And he added, "What else is there? That is it. Tell them if they give their lives to Christ, they will find life." (Excerpt from a sermon titled "Now Is the Time to Live," by Norman Vincent Peale. Copyright 1977. Used by permission from Foundation of Christian Living.)

I'm moved every time I read that statement. It makes me understand why the influence of preacher Peale's son has been so powerful. How wise he was to counsel him to stick with the basics of loving people and calling them to know Christ.

I end this book with a personal word to every Christian communicator. It matters not to me whether you preach the gospel from the pulpit, teach the truth in a classroom, or make known the good news of God's love on a one-to-one basis. The thing that matters is that we all understand the secret of success isn't so much in our heads as in our hearts. Before we can powerfully present Christ we must experience the Pentecostal presence that makes us witnesses in our world.

The strategies and styles of our ministries may be changed by the times. But it will always be true that the world we witness to will never care how much we know until they know how much we care.

Robert Raikes probably wasn't the smartest man in Gloucester back in 1780. But he cared more than most. And that's why we honor him today as the founder of the modern Sunday school movement.

In the final analysis, the eternal difference is made more by the fire in our hearts than by the facts in our heads.